MY STORY OF ADOPTING
THREE CHILDREN FROM HAITI

# BOTH ENDS
# BURNING

## CRAIG JUNTUNEN

**Outskirts Press, Inc.**
**Denver, Colorado**

# Table of Contents

# Dedication

This book is dedicated to the orphaned and abandoned children of this world.

# Author's Notes for the Second Edition

*Both Ends Burning* is a story of hope, proving that if children receive love, support, and direction, they have a chance to actualize the greatness inside them.

As their proud father, I consider Amelec, Espie and Quinn to be exceptional. As an advocate for international adoption, I know they are simply representative of the world's orphan epidemic. I wrote this book to inspire others to consider the possibility of international adoption. Once you have read this story you will know that international adoption works, when it happens. Sadly, as the years go on, it is happening less and less.

International adoption is in crisis. From 2004 to 2009, adoptions into the U.S. declined by more than 45 percent. During that same period, the number of orphaned and abandoned children in the world has grown. The orphaned and abandoned children of Haiti, as in other desperate parts of the world, were simply born into dreadful circumstances. There are millions of kids in the world who were dealt a bad hand at birth, and are struggling to stay alive. These children would be great additions to any family, and that realization offered me plenty of motivation to write this book and to advocate on their behalf.

As I write these notes for the Second Edition, it has been almost four years since our kids arrived with us at the Phoenix airport. Of the many lessons I have learned in that time, these two stand out from the rest: (1) kids are kids, whether they were born in Houston or Haiti; and, (2) the system of international adoption is broken.

I am committed to changing the scene of international adoption. Both ends of the adoption spectrum are burning: Families who want to adopt are blocked, and children who need a home are being denied that chance. In response to this crisis I have started a foundation called the Both Ends Burning Campaign, which is on the web at www.bothendsburning.org. The royalties from your purchase of this edition of my book will be directed to the foundation, a broad-based campaign to reverse the declining trend in international adoptions and bring some sensibility into the process so that more orphans and families can be connected.

I hope you enjoy this book. If you do not, I hope you will find some consolation in the fact that a portion of your purchase price went to support the efforts to persuade the world that adoption is a good thing to do, and to transform the process so more kids will have a future filled with possibilities and options.

I wrote the book from my heart and have attempted to provide you with an honest retelling of my thoughts and feelings. I have changed a few of the names for privacy reasons. I hope you appreciate the spirit behind these words.

Craig Juntunen, June 1, 2010

# Chapter 1

## Never Say Never

I had a vasectomy when I was 30.

To put that portion of my medical history into context, what I was doing was swearing off kids at an early age, clearly seeing them as a distraction to where I was going. My aim in life was simple: work hard while I figured out the game, then once I understood the game, work the game as fast as I could and retire at 40. From my perspective, kids certainly added no value into that equation.

As odd as it seems, my vasectomy became part of my identity as I reentered the dating scene after the end of my marriage in 1988. The minor medical procedure had more than minor ramifications for how I was perceived by the women I began to date. To me, it was no big deal since I never, ever considered having kids. It was a 25-minute procedure on a Friday afternoon that just as well could have been the removal of a wart.

I arrived at the doctor's office right on time, 1:30 p.m. The waiting room was typical of any doctor's office -- stark and tidy, with a familiar hint of medical antiseptic in the air. There were a couple of lamps in the corners and a few worn-out magazines on the coffee table. The atmosphere perfectly reflected my expectations this would be a routine procedure. When I arrived I sat near two other men who appeared a lot older -- and more fidgety -- than I. They were uneasy, as if forced to walk the plank on a pirate ship with a gun to their head. The gaze in their eyes started to make me anxious. Did they know something I didn't?

That was the extent of the time I had to scrutinize my fellow waiting room mates, for as soon as I sat down my name was called. The receptionist who led me into the room was blond and cute, very wholesome, the kind of a girl your mom would want you to marry. I half-heartedly wondered if her presence here was intentional, a strategic plant representing one last-ditch effort to get me to rethink what I was about to do. Turns out, I didn't have time to ask, as she turned right around without any eye contact. "The doctor will be right with you," she said in a businesslike tone. She closed the door abruptly behind her.

I was left alone in a small room at the end of the hall for 15 minutes, which again could have been construed as some moral or ethical ploy to have me reconsider what I was about to do. But I prevailed over such thoughts. This was not about morals or ethics; it was for me a pragmatic lifestyle decision. Frankly, the only tangible concern looming over me was whether my mechanical parts would still work once this was over. I had been very clear in all previous conversations with the doctor that I did not want this procedure interfering with any of my currently functioning anatomy. I had been assured that this would have no effect on all the moving parts I considered important. I took that guarantee at face value. I patiently waited and my thoughts drifted until I heard footsteps approach the door.

"Mr. Juntunen, my name is Dr. Franklin and I will be doing your procedure this afternoon. This is my assistant Hilda and she will be supporting me."

Hilda was not nearly as attractive as the cute receptionist. Dr. Franklin said he needed to do a quick check of the area and then we would be on our way. He sounded like a pilot addressing his passengers right before takeoff. His demeanor was very formal and official, which comforted me, considering he was about to utilize sharp scissors on a very important part of my body. After a few routine "Umms and aahhhs" directed at Hilda, he said we could proceed.

As he began to go to work, Dr. Franklin announced I was the first patient he had seen on a Friday afternoon who showed up sober. Most men down a few cocktails to deal with their apprehension about getting a vasectomy, he said. This insight might have explained the behavior of the two other patients who still waited in the lobby. Sober and game, I took a deep breath and we were on our way.

A couple of tiny incisions and 25 minutes later, and that was that. Done.

I hadn't felt a thing. Nor did I feel any different. Pants and zipper up, and I was on my way. I drove myself home, hoping that they had told me the truth when they said that all parts would be up and running again in a few days. By the time I got to the first stoplight I realized a portion of my future was now formally defined. There was finality to what I had just done. Any chance of becoming a dad had been tied up in an examination room at the northern end of a grey office complex. By the time I had arrived at the next stoplight, I had stopped thinking about it. Moving on from what had just happened was as easy as passing through the changing stoplights.

However, this turned out not to be an open and shut case for the women I dated thereafter. In one way or another, it mattered to them. A vasectomy for a divorced man in his early thirties, smack dab in the middle of the dating scene, is a very sharp double-edged sword. Discovery of my altered plumbing was inevitable and, for the most part, the reaction was surprisingly intense. Once the subject came up--and it always did--my date would either see me as a prudent and sensible man who understood his priorities (followed by a sigh of relief acknowledging that I couldn't get her pregnant), or, more frequently, a hyperventilating look of shock, as if she were watching me peel away a mask exposing the hideous and contorted face I had been hiding. When that happened there was no need for a follow-up conversation. The date's irregular breathing pattern meant she felt there was something wrong with me because of my decision to eliminate the possibility of ever having kids.

The practical problem became when to tell them, as many of them desired children and more than a few had begun to pencil me in as the father of their future children even before the dessert cart showed up. And, when the news finally fell into the conversation, a wall of tension went up since many believed I had deceived them from the beginning. One of them remarked: "Gosh, you don't look like a guy who would have intentionally mutilated himself at such an early age."

Now, it wasn't always bad news. A couple of women I dated found it comforting. They saw this as the perfect out and they were now free to not take me seriously. Just because I was now stricken from their long-term prospect list didn't mean we couldn't have a little fun along the way. We stopped trying to impress each other knowing we had no "real future" together. Being together for a while for the fun of it became just that, fun. While my controversial decision was a difficulty for some of my dates, it was never a source of confusion for me. I never wavered or doubted, not even for a moment.

Kathi started out like all of the rest. A passing glance, a shy hello, a few awkward pleasantries that led me to ask her out to lunch. For three years prior to meeting her I could have been described as an extreme dater -- a fact that had expanded my experience of other human beings, something which had only left me more jaded. And yet another byproduct of my constant dating was that my instincts became a trusted friend. From the minute I met Kathi my instincts told me a lot about her, and I listened to them. I saw her as an honest, decent and sincere person, qualities that were rare within my dating portfolio.

Inspired by her unique characteristics, I decided to employ a new disclosure strategy with her. I decided to go ahead and tell her right off the bat. Boom! Get it over with and see where the chips fell. Whatever the outcome,

I was proud of the tactical decision, and I could see it might have some long term positive ramifications for my overall dating efficiency. As soon as we ordered lunch I began to tell her.

"You should know that I am never going to get married again..." followed by, "I had a vasectomy, which means I can't and never will have kids ..." and to make sure I covered all bases I added, "Don't count on me ever sending you flowers, because I don't believe in that."

Once I had made all my declarations, she stared at me with the most beautiful steel blue eyes. The look wasn't a look I had seen before -- it was lacking in the incredulous, shocked expression. Frankly, my speech had not come out as well as when I had practiced it earlier in the car. I was a little embarrassed as I waited for her to pronounce verdict. At first I thought my candor would create some sort of win-win scenario with her, believing she would appreciate my honesty, but the bluntness of it made me willing to settle for a break-even. As I emotionally backtracked, I began hoping to dodge any comparison to Jack the Ripper.

"That is a little more information than I really need to know at this time, Craig," she politely replied, not even blinking. Calm, anything but shocked. Still breathing regularly.

I had had worse reactions. A lot worse. This was promising.

In retrospect, I probably had gone too far with the "no flowers" comment. I thought it would fit in nicely with my new "full disclosure" strategy and besides, at the time, it was the truth. In any event, she was able to look past the faulty timing of my unusual announcements and somehow I did enough other things right to convince her to give me another look with Date Number Two.

She moved in with me six months later.

We married a year to the day after I sold my company and became financially set for life. We had become best friends and were committed to spending the rest of our years enjoying each other, traveling the world and living the good life. And for the record I did send her flowers, enough times to be classified as sentimental.

I had gotten very lucky on a number of fronts. I had sold my business for a very good price and, along the way, had married a saint. Over the years I can't tell you how many times I thought to myself what a great mom she would have made. But as fate would have it, luck was not on her side, since she had married me -- the Never-Dad. My vasectomy was irreversible.

Maybe the story I am about to tell you is proof you should never say never. Life is far too unpredictable. More than a decade and a half since my declaration at lunch, there I was with Kathi standing on a steamy tarmac in Port-Au-Prince, Haiti, about to board a plane with Amelec, Esperancia and Quinn -- three children. Our children.

As we shuffled toward the stairs that would lead us up to the plane I looked down at their anxious faces. I was staring right down into the barrel of my future. The truth was, I didn't know if I had thrown my life away or if I was going to learn about love the hard way. We all held hands walking to the stairs of the plane, gripping a sense of uncertainty. The only certainty was that, once the wheels of this plane were up, there was no turning back.

At 51, I had become a dad.

# Chapter 2

## Last Straw

It was either a yoga teacher or some other self-help expert I once dated who told me I had trouble living in the moment. There was more than a speck of truth to that observation. When I was in grade school, my sights were on getting to high school. Once in high school, I couldn't get to college fast enough. When I got to college, I couldn't wait to enter the real world and get a job. And, of course, once I got a job, I could only think of one thing, retirement.

My goal in life was to retire by the time I was 40. I don't know why I put that arbitrary stake in the ground, but I did. I now believe one of life's greatest tricks is the allure of retirement. We assume that in retirement we will be free of all of the things that make us miserable when we were working. I sacrificed plenty to grow a company and sell it towards the end of my 40th year. There were plenty of trade-offs in that proposition and, in the end, all that was delivered was a bucket full of boredom. "Love and work ... work and love, that's all there is," said Sigmund Freud. Turns out dropping one of those has a negative effect on the other. Once you retire, because you are not working, the person you love becomes so sick and tired of the constant contact that life's equation suddenly adds up to a big fat zero.

I had my own company in the 1990s, which turned out to be a great way to get rich. It was a human capital consulting company, headquartered in San Francisco and serving the major technology markets across the country. For anyone who was paying attention, being included in the technology boom from 1980 to 2000 was like owning a lottery ticket with really good odds of winning. I held one of those winning tickets. I was right in the middle of the boom and its powerful undertow yanked my company in the right direction.

My ticket got punched in October 1995. I had hit the jackpot. It all happened so fast. We had been grinding it out, just plugging along, and then one day, I looked up and our performance record told the story of an incredibly successful company. The business wasn't for sale on the open market, but I received three different offers that year. I took the last offer and the deal gave me more money than I could reasonably spend for the rest of my life.

I was done. Work game over -- next game, retirement. I could go anywhere, live anywhere and do anything. I chose to move to Vail, Colorado, for the skiing and the golf, and, even though it violated one of my few commandments, I asked Kathi to marry me.

Initially my retirement was a perpetual grand vacation. The stress of the business was gone and I didn't have to listen to unhappy customers or crybaby employees and I woke up every morning giggling. After the years of sacrifice and commitment we traveled to places we'd dreamed of seeing. We stayed in the finest hotels and dined in some of the best restaurants in the world. We were living large. Kathi's conservative and practical nature reminded me of how fortunate we were: One night after the two of us had a sumptuous dinner in Monte Carlo, she remarked shyly, "I can't believe we just did that," as we walked up the steps to the entrance of a casino.

Even though we traveled first class to many premier destinations in the world, we were more comfortable being at home. I took long walks in the morning with my dogs when the only sound was the wind rushing through pines on the vast slopes of the Rockies. Our two yellow labs, Buster and Bubba, led the way as I walked down a wooded path to a small stream near our home. I splashed crisp, clear water on my face and the three of us -- retired man and two dogs -- sat on the water's edge and watched the sun come up over the mountains.

My dream had come true. I had found freedom.

In the first year of retirement I discovered a peaceful independence that was everything I had dreamed it would be. The feeling joined me on those walks with my dogs, and the yoga teacher I used to date wouldn't have recognized me -- I was finally living in the moment. We resided in a country club golf community in Colorado and bought another home in Scottsdale, Arizona, also in a golf community made up of people like us. All our time was spent recreating. We golfed in Arizona in the spring and fall, hiked the Rockies in the summer, and skied and snow-shoed the mountains in the winter. During that time the toughest decisions I faced were whether to use a driver or a three-wood off the tee, and whether to drink red or white wine with dinner. Life couldn't have been easier.

We also undertook the obligation to give some of our good fortune back. I took the easy way out: I wrote checks. Kathi, on the other hand, made a commitment to get involved with some of the projects we financially supported, rolling up her sleeves and investing sweat equity into a variety of causes. Led by her heart and humanity, I joined her in looking for programs to be a part of. These missions all mattered and made sense to us, but while it was easy for us to become sympathetic to these causes, we weren't passionate about them. It is not that they lacked significance, we just could not emotionally connect with them the way we thought we should.

Aside from the occasional giving back part, our retirement life was a very self-serving existence. Our lifestyle was very social -- something that was problematic for my introverted nature. Kathi made plenty of new friends and I simply tagged along. Since no one in either community really had much to do, we all hung out together; playing golf or skiing during the day, then at night climbing onto the cocktail and dinner party carousel. Everyone took turns having the evening shindig at their house and attempted to "one up" the party from the night before. All of us who had the arrow of good fortune fall down on them now formed one big clique.

What else were we going to do?

In a way, we had gone full circle back to the college lifestyle of revolving parties, except now there was a huge expansion in the party budget. Cheap beer kegs had been replaced by champagne fountains and aged red wine, but I soon learned a high-end cocktail party shares many similarities with a frat-house kegger.

I have never been one for cocktail party banter. Could I have entertaining and meaningful conversations with the same people night after night? No one put a gun to our head to go to these parties, but Kathi's philosophy was that if we are going to live in these communities we should make the effort to be a part of them. She understood my social inadequacies and thought it was good for me to get out of my comfort zone and interact with others to keep my mind stimulated. She was right about one thing: I was definitely out of my comfort zone. In fact, I was usually miserable trying to chitchat about nothing in particular. And it did very little to keep my mind stimulated.

But for the most part Kathi seemed to be enjoying herself so I could, at least, suck it up and be a good sport. I was still pinching myself about the price I had received for my company and, for the time being, any effort to attend these parties was really incidental. During the early days of retirement I simply discounted them as my least favorite part of a really great lifestyle.

While it was a stretch for me to tolerate the social part of the country club lifestyle, I loved the golfing part. The golf course became my new office and I gladly showed up everyday. I played with the same circle of friends at the clubs that I belonged to. The camaraderie, the competition, the challenge of a very demanding game brought me back to the first tee every day. If golf is addictive, then I was an addict.

But sometimes addicts lose their craving.

One morning I was standing on the first tee box with three of my frequent golf buddies. On that beautiful summer morning, with the grass sparkling from the morning dew, I stared down the first fairway and I asked myself, "Is this how it is going to be? … Is this all that my life has become?" I had no idea where the thought came from, but on that picture perfect morning I had been hit by an emotional stun gun. I was shaken to the core by what had just crossed my mind.

I quickly countered in an attempt to reassure myself. "Hey, it doesn't get any better than this! Get up there and hit your tee shot!" But as I entered the tee box the thought returned.

"There has to be more to life than this," nagged at me. Dazed and rattled by my internal debate, I did my best to try to hit the ball down the middle of the fairway. Golf gives a player plenty of time to think about things in between shots. I just couldn't get the feeling out of my head. There was a melancholy mood settling into me. At first I considered these thoughts to be a personal betrayal. How in the world could I be questioning any of this? I had made it! This was the life I had sacrificed so much for and for so many years. This was the big reward for the extraordinarily long work weeks, the thousands of miles of travel, and all the other stresses that come with owning a business.

But that morning on the golf course was the first moment the big reward felt a little different. Now my confusion went beyond the inconsequential and trivial nature of the parties Kathi kept dragging me to. This was different; in questioning my relationship with golf, I was questioning something deeper, something that mattered to me.

The retirement honeymoon -- which had been standing perfectly on a pedestal I had built -- suddenly had a crack in it.

Over the next few years, my disdain for the cocktail party circuit grew, which, given my personality, was predictable. What wasn't predictable was how my love affair with golf began to fade. My feelings were hard to explain. I was trying to cope with a personal mutiny and I was disillusioned and confused about the emotional tailspin. Even in the midst of having everything, life was becoming a struggle. As the days passed, my whining about having to show up for another dinner party got a little louder.

* * *

Another night, another party. The beautiful stone house was the size of a small hotel. As Kathi and I parked, it appeared we were the last to arrive. I grabbed the bottle of wine that was neatly tucked into a frilly rectangular wine bag that Kathi had selected from the dozen or so bags we had in the pantry. In this neighborhood, simply bringing a bottle of wine to your host and hostess wasn't enough; it had to be dressed up and presented in a fancy designer bag. I never really understood why we all did this. The dinner party custom was simply a rotation of the same people at houses which all had their own massive wine cellars. It would have been much simpler and more efficient if we had all just skipped the obligatory "show up gift" and called it even. But we didn't.

Another tedious part of the ritual was the house tour. Retired people with a ton of money and not much else to do take a lot of pride in the grand houses they build and fill with things. To be honest, Kathi and I had given our fair share of house tours, something I am not proud of now. Who cares about the size and opulence of your home?

We had never been to this particular house and that meant we were on the radar as tour prospects. Sure enough, once we entered the beautiful foyer the hostess hustled over to greet us. Even though she told everyone this was just a casual get-together, she was dressed like royalty, looking like she expected a film crew to show up at any minute. I wore a denim shirt with a little football helmet logo on it, which seemed out of place with her stunning and formal attire. We offered our fancy bag of wine and I waited for the unavoidable.

"Welcome to our little get-together, we have been wanting to have you over to see the place for some time. Would you like to look around?" she asked. "We would love to show you some of the fun things our design team came up with."

Kathi would have clobbered me if I had told the truth.

"Oh sure, we would love to see what you have done, we have heard so much about it," Kathi said, validating that she has better manners and more social grace than I do.

As we were escorted through the staged and

magnificent home I wondered how many more of these "tours" my shaken disposition could take. It annoyed me we all felt compelled to share the story behind our bathroom faucets. I asked myself, "Couldn't some of this tremendous creative energy be applied in a different and more meaningful direction?"

While I had seen plenty of spectacular houses, this one was over the top. We wound our way through a maze of hand-carved woodwork and imported 18th century marble. When we entered the walk-in closet, which was the size of a studio apartment, the hostess pointed out the built-in dry cleaning unit in the corner. I asked if it really worked and she looked at me as if I were just trying to be cute. We finished the tour by passing a 2,000-bottle wine cellar that was lined with wood imported from a remote region in Chile. Finally, we were unleashed to join the rest of the guests in the bar.

The good news was we had been liberated from the tour. The bad news was that this night was an "assigned seating night." I knew this to be a common strategy that hostesses used to force their guests to mix. It really meant I was not going to get to sit with my golf buddies and, most likely would end up next to someone with whom I had nothing in common.

Just as I had feared, I didn't get a favorable draw with the dinner seating and wound up perched between two women I had met previously but didn't know very well. The two of them plunged into conversation, with me sandwiched between them. That was fine; at least I didn't have to say much.

I don't think either of them got the note this was supposed to be a casual affair either, as one was sporting a prom night hairdo and way too much makeup, and the other had sequins on two of the three primary items that made up her outfit. During the salad course, they discussed the perplexities of designer jeans and how one of them had such a difficult time finding just the right fit because of her extraordinarily long inseam.

As ridiculous and tormenting the inseam discussion was, they continued to top it as the other dinner courses were served. By the time dessert came they had become very disappointed I wasn't blown away by the fact that they both had unknowingly bought the same rare china from different distributors.

Except for the food and the wine, the evening was torture, and when the plates were finally cleared, I breathed the same sigh of relief I breathe when a dentist says, "We're finished." We were the first to leave and, at first, Kathi didn't understand why I was in such a hurry to get out of there. Granted, she did have a different seat at the table.

While it had been a privilege to be included in the evening, I had lost that feeling of honor sometime between the designer jean crisis and the one-of-a-kind china fiasco. I had just been in one of the most spectacular homes I had ever seen, I had been served a five-star meal with accompanying five-star wines, and not counting the superfluous bottle of wine we brought, I hadn't paid a thing for the evening. By anybody's standard it was a lavish and extravagant evening. But sometime during the night's festivities, I had been served the straw that broke the camel's back.

That was the gist of it. It was over for me. Once we buckled up in the car I turned to Kathi and told her that if this evening were a foreshadowing of the rest of my life, I should just go ahead and end it right now because I couldn't take it anymore.

She looked at me with those eyes I had loved from the minute I met her and said quietly, "Me too."

The retirement honeymoon had fallen off its perfect pedestal, hit the ground, and shattered into a million meaningless pieces.

# Chapter 3

## Inspiration

Depending on how you look at things, what happened next was either the result of divine intervention or a great coincidence. In either case, the life Kathi and I were questioning was about to radically change.

Some of life's most significant moments occur when you don't know they are happening. One day, I received an email from an acquaintance asking if I wanted to join him and a friend for a round of golf. I knew Rick socially, but we had never played golf together. He had a great reputation and was seen as a leader in our community. He seemed like the kind of guy I should get to know better, and there is no better place to get to know someone than on the golf course. I was flattered by his invitation and replied I would see him in the morning.

Rick and I were about the same age, but when he

greeted me on the driving range, his vitality and energy made him appear younger than me. He is a full-of-life Italian-American, who talks with his hands and charms you with his smile. And there was a sincerity to him I found very appealing. The three of us were the only guys at the club that morning and we decided to start on the back nine. We all hit good tee shots and Rick and I walked down the left side of the fairway with our caddies right behind us. As we continued to get more acquainted, we exchanged information about our personal lives. The account of my family lasted a few steps; I told him I was married to the greatest girl in the world, and that was the end of it. I could have thrown in the fact that we also owned two very large and ill-behaved dogs, but I felt that was just padding the conversation.

On the other hand, Rick needed many more steps to tell me about his family. He and his wife, Peggy, had raised three boys, one now in college and two in the professional world. He told me about some of their accomplishments and, based on that, he certainly had a right to be a proud father. I could tell that his family meant a lot to him by the tone of his voice, and I was impressed by his passion as he spoke about his kids.

We arrived at his ball for his second shot, and in the same breath that he had asked Robbie, his caddie, for his six iron, Rick added, "And a year ago we adopted two girls from Haiti," then addressed his ball and fired a six-iron into the middle of the green.

It was a very good shot, but I was too taken by what he had just told me to fully acknowledge it. As I watched his ball in flight, I realized I wasn't exactly sure where Haiti was located. And I was pretty sure that I had never met anyone who had adopted children. I missed the green with my shot and we split up to approach our respective balls.

Part of my nature is that I am very inquisitive. That may be one of the traits that made me successful in business, and I had a reputation for conducting a tough but interesting interview. As I tracked down my errant shot, I had plenty of questions for Rick: Why Haiti? Why these two girls? Why did you and your wife adopt in the first place? What is different in raising these two girls from the experience of raising your biological children?

Because I had hit such a lousy second shot I was on the other side of the green, a long way from my playing partners. I hit my chip tight to the hole and as we all marked our balls preparing to line up our putts, I turned to Rick and asked: "Do they call you Dad?"

I stared at him waiting for his response. As he crouched down to replace his ball he looked up at me and started to tear up. "Yes, they do."

I could see in his eyes his affection for his children, even though they were not his biological kids. I found his response remarkable.

Desert golf is very unforgiving, and a bad shot usually means your ball cohabitates with prickly cactus, gnarly scrub brush, and, occasionally, rattlesnakes. On the third hole, Rick snap-hooked his tee shot into the desert and the three of us and the caddies began to rummage around looking for his ball. As we all shuffled along hoping to spot a speck of white in the dust of the desert I shouted out to Rick, "Why Haiti?" without taking my eyes off the treacherous landscape.

My outburst disrupted everyone's concentration and

all I heard back was a faint, "What?"

"Why Haiti?" I repeated, again without looking up.

Rick had now drifted beside me and he stopped searching for his ball. "Think of the worst place you have ever seen. Haiti is much worse than that. For the record, it is the poorest country in the Western Hemisphere, but that does not accurately describe it. Hundreds of thousands of kids literally are starving to death. Bad water, no food. It is hard to say what is going to kill them first, dehydration or starvation."

His statement was piercing. He was so adamant. So convictive.

We gave up looking for his ball and somberly returned back to the plush fairway. Now that we were back onto the safety of grass, he looked me sternly in the eyes and said, "If you saw what we saw you would understand why we were compelled to adopt these two kids. There are close to a million orphaned or abandoned kids in Haiti today." And then he added without hesitation, "Probably should have adopted more."

Golf seemed pretty insignificant right about then and it was difficult for me to focus on anything other than his experience in Haiti. I asked questions persistently, perhaps annoying him through the rest of the round, although I held off when we were looking for someone's ball in the desert.

I wondered about all the kids he was describing and how lucky his two girls were. I was just about to putt on hole number 12, but I couldn't concentrate, thinking about the fortune or fate that had intervened for these two girls. I just had to ask, "How did you find them?"

"Modern technology. There are tons of agencies that

specialize in international adoption. Peggy did all of the work and had selected a short list of agencies. We saw a photo of these two sisters on a web page. I was captivated by the brilliance and sparkle in their eyes. The instant I saw them I told Peggy this was something we needed to pursue. We flew down to meet them a few weeks later. Meeting them was something I will never forget - that meeting compelled us to adopt them."

I wondered why someone who had dedicated so much of his life to raising kids would turn around and do it again. Then I asked the last question of the round. We were walking up the 18th fairway and I was running out of real estate to conduct my interrogation.

"Is it different? I mean, from raising your own kids?"

"They are our own kids and I feel just like I did with the first three. There has never been any confusion about that."

"It feels the same, really?" I challenged.

"Parenting is parenting. I loved it the first time, and the fact of the matter is I am doing a better job of parenting now than I did with the boys. Most of that is because I have more experience this time around. I am older and I learned from some of the mistakes that I made. Peggy likes to refer to us as second-generation parents. I am having a ball with these kids and I hate to say it, but parenting is a little more fun at this stage in my life."

The phrase "little more fun" struck a nerve, especially since chronic boredom had taken up permanent residence in my life. I was impressed with what Rick and Peggy had done and there was an overriding sensibility to their noble action. It seemed so significant and so simple at the same time. Choosing to reach out and literally save the lives of these kids made so much sense to me. I wondered to myself, why don't more people do this? How hard can it be? And then to my amazement, as I was walking off the 18th green, I found myself thinking, why don't Kathi and I do this?

The round of golf was over and a catharsis was brewing. I was more than curious about the subjects of Haiti and international adoption, and I was anxious to learn more. On top of that I had just shot a smooth 76. It was time for a beer.

Rick's friend had to leave so that left the two of us for the traditional after-the-round drink. Earlier I had been impressed with Rick for his professional accomplishments. Now, after spending the last four hours with him, I admired his character and his humility. He didn't have to go to the trouble of adopting those kids from Haiti; he did it simply because he saw it as the right thing to do.

I was soaking it all in. I was fascinated with details of his trips to Haiti and his descriptions of a place I could hardly imagine. Rick and Peggy had made a number of trips to Haiti to begin the bonding process with their two girls while they waited for the paperwork to formalize the adoption. He told me he had seen mothers make mud pies and place them on the hot streets to "cook" them for lunch and dinner. He told me of a priest they had met on one of the trips.

His name was Father Tom Hagan. He had moved to Haiti in 1995 and started an organization called Hands Together in Cite Soleil, a district in the Haitian capital, Port-Au-Prince. Cite Soleil has the reputation of being the poorest and most violent slum in the world, Rick said.

Murder, kidnapping and rapes are daily occurrences. Father Tom walked away from his life in the United States to try to make a difference in a very bad place. He has chosen to live in what is clearly one of the worst places in the world to live.

On that note, we finished our beers and it was time to go home. I was sorry to see this golf day end. We walked out to the turn-around and waited for the valet to bring our cars. I didn't have the words to describe how much I had enjoyed Rick's company and this particular round of golf. I just shook his hand, looked him in the eye, and muttered, "Thanks, see you soon."

Endings are just precursors for beginnings. I didn't know it at the time but that day was the beginning of a new life for Kathi and me. As I drove home I kept thinking about Haiti and how so many kids were suffering there. I thought of the privileged and sheltered lifestyle I was living today and how different it was from the way people in Haiti were living. I was so deep in thought I almost missed the turn up the hill to my house. A line in a song on the radio haunted me: "All you touch and all you see is all your life will ever be." I turned the radio off and drove up the hill, lost in thought.

When I got home, I asked Kathi to make dinner reservations -- we had something to talk about. I went straight to my office to get on the computer and looked up everything I could find about Father Tom Hagan. I read about some of the things Rick had told me. The inspiring story of Father Tom and the awful conditions of Cite Soleil mesmerized me.

I spent the remainder of the afternoon reading articles on the Internet and thinking about Rick and Father Tom. I considered what they were doing ... and what I wasn't doing. I reminded myself that life could be reduced to the sum of the decisions that you make. I started thinking about decisions and sacrifices. At this point in my life what, if anything, had I left to give? I speculated what it would be like to experience a place like Cite Soleil, even only for a few days. I was in a trance when Kathi knocked on my office door to tell me we were going to be late for dinner. I told her I needed to do just one more thing and I would be right there.

I pulled out the atlas from my bookcase. I figured if I was going to Haiti, I at least ought to know where it is.

* * *

Between the 14th and 17th holes I had decided to go to Haiti. If you had asked me why then, I wouldn't have been able to tell you. Something Rick said had gotten under my skin, and I was motivated to do something I couldn't explain. I was going to tell Kathi at dinner that night, and I was assuming it would be hard for her to understand, because even I didn't understand it. She had made reservations at our favorite Italian restaurant, and we were seated at a corner table out on the veranda. I told her right after the waiter poured water into our glasses.

"I'm thinking about taking a trip to Haiti," I said as routinely as if I had said I was thinking about going to the bathroom. She took her eyes off the sunset and looked at me as if she had not quite understood. There was an uncomfortable few seconds of silence and I started to repeat myself, but before I could, she squinted, scrunched her nose, and said, "Haiti?"

"Yes, Haiti," I said, already on the defensive.

She looked perplexed as she stared back at me, focusing on my need for approval. She had stopped squinting. Knowing I am not the adventurous type, she only needed one word to reply to my news.

"Why?"

"It is a long story that I just heard over a four-hour round of golf. I don't think dinner will last that long, so I will try to give you the short version."

She pushed her chair slightly away from the table and leaned back. "Take your time."

I began to retell the story of what Rick and Peggy had done. I told her my motivation was fueled by Rick's passionate description of a dismal place. I replayed his explanation of a nation in a tailspin. Haiti's infrastructure had all but collapsed, and political corruption had brought the country into a state of chaos. Fifteen percent of the population was orphaned or abandoned children, and most wandered the streets, struggling to survive. Without missing a beat I also told her what I had read about Father Tom and how I wanted to meet him. I was on a roll -- but she cut me off.

"Craig, let me get this straight. You, being one of the least religious people I know, are telling me that you want to go to someplace you know nothing about, to meet a priest you have just read about on the Internet this afternoon?" she stuttered and stammered. "This is…This is…This is not like you at all. This does not add up. Haiti? A priest? You?"

I wasn't sure if she was confused, angry, or scared. I did my best to try to clarify things. "I know it sounds crazy, honey, but there is something tugging at me, and I wish I could describe it so it would make sense to you, or even make sense to me."

She looked baffled. This had gotten off to a very bad start. But all I could do was continue on with my feeble attempt at an explanation. "Haiti is the antithesis of this," I said spreading my arms out to the lights of metropolitan Phoenix. That pitch missed.

I went on trying desperately to make some sense of the situation. "Haiti is in stark contrast to the life I know, and, I might add, a life I am not all that crazy about right now. My gut is telling me I need to go and do this. And you know I don't really care if Father Tom is or isn't a priest. What I find interesting is that he has decided to live in the worst slum in the world, trying to make it a better place. Shaking hands with a guy who is willing to make that kind of a sacrifice could only make my life better. Think about it, the worst slum in the world. This trip could change my life, or at least my perspective of life."

By the look in her eyes I could tell she was still a doubter. She knew I hadn't really thought it all through. Kathi responds better to fact than emotion and maybe that is why this was getting off to such a rocky start. My recent look at the atlas could help start a new tone for this conversation.

"And, it would be an easy trip. It is only 500 miles off the coast of Florida, right next to Cuba. I don't know what carrier flies there, but it can't be anymore than an hour and a half flight from Miami."

Demonstrating knowledge of this geographical fact was also an attempt to show I was serious. I was banking on this supporting data to help refute the look in her eyes that said I was just having a boredom-induced fantasy.

Instead, things went from bad to worse. "The last I checked, Haiti doesn't have a Ritz-Carlton," she taunted.

That was a low blow, and she knew it. I didn't even attempt to answer and she backed down. Her guilt, combined with my impressive 500-mile stat, calmed the conversation, and Kathi shifted gears. She started asking questions. "What kind of shots or medical preparations do you have to take prior to going?"

That was one of many details I hadn't yet considered, but I wasn't ready to discuss travel arrangements just yet. I just wanted to share with her my newfound sense of adventure. I quickly tried to circle the conversation back to the potential for a life-altering experience.

"I will go to the doctor this week and I am sure they can tell me about shots."

"What about.... where you are going to stay?.... And how are you ...."

I cut her off in mid-sentence, a little aggravated she was focusing on minutiae. I knew the details could all be worked out -- they always get worked out. This was about something much bigger, and I was a little annoyed she wanted to bring the conversation down to a sensible level.

"Honey, I don't know all of the practical ramifications. I don't know where I am staying or how I am getting there -- haven't even thought about it. I am just telling you that this is something that I am going to do." I said it firmly enough that the point was finally made.

She understood. She had known me long enough to sense I had made up my mind even though there were a lot more questions than answers as we picked away at our salads.

There was a lengthy period of silence as we both rehashed the conversation in our minds. I was still a little put off by her Ritz-Carlton comment. She broke the silence. "There is one more thing that you need to consider."

"What is that?" I said with more than a little irritation in my voice.

"Is there room for one more? Because I am going with you."

# Chapter 4

## A Hell-Hole Called Haiti

We spent the rest of the dinner talking about *our* trip and we held hands on the short car ride home. There were plenty of details and arrangements to be made. But that was always Kathi's department. I was just excited she was going to join me on this journey and, though I had made up my mind earlier to do this, everything now felt a little more defined. As I pulled into our driveway and waited for our gate to open I felt a sense of certainty in going to a very uncertain place.

Over the next couple of days I found time to do a little more research. I learned Haiti shares the island of Hispaniola in the Caribbean with the Dominican Republic. By all accounts, Haiti seems to have gotten the short end of the stick. First of all, it didn't even get its fair share of the land: Haiti occupies only one-third of the island. And on the island of Hispaniola, bigger is better.

The Dominican Republic is not exactly an economic juggernaut, but compared to Haiti, it resembles a world superpower.

Haiti was one of the first countries to face the AIDS epidemic, and as a consequence, its tourism industry collapsed. Meanwhile, the Dominican Republic has enough tourism to support a modest but growing economy.

According to accounts I read on the Internet, Haiti is a country that is in a constant state of social and political convulsion. Its economy is in ruins. Four out of ten adults cannot read or write. Half of the households are forced to live on less than one dollar a day. Eighty percent of Haitians do not have access to clean drinking water. Haiti has the highest rate of AIDS, malnutrition and infant mortality in the region.

Rick had not exaggerated. From my research, Haiti was a hell-hole. But as hopeless as the conditions there appeared to be, I found something appealing about the island nation. Maybe it was my affinity for the underdog. Whatever the reason, I was curious about a lifestyle that was grueling and demanding. The more I learned, the more fascinated I became. I have lived my life as a contrarian, and everything I was consuming about Haiti made it more alluring to me.

First thing Monday morning Kathi called our doctor and unbelievably we were able to get an appointment that day. Getting in to see a doctor in Scottsdale the same day you call is about as a likely as a snowstorm in Phoenix. We entered the standing-room only waiting area five minutes early for our 3:45 appointment. It appeared whoever had booked our appointment was on a commission plan and had drastically overbooked the doctor's time. At 4:35 a nurse finally called our names.

It was Kathi who boldly announced to the doctor we were going to Haiti, and we needed the necessary vaccines.

"Haiti!" he exclaimed, "Why in the world are you guys going there?"

We were then an hour past our appointment time and I was not in the mood to socialize, so I skipped sharing any of my deep-seated theories of why I wanted to do it. "Ah, it is just something we want to do," I said plainly, leaving it at that.

I probably should have responded with more of a conversational approach, as it was clear he disapproved of the idea, and launched a crusade to talk us out of it. "I wouldn't go to Haiti if I were you. In fact, there are a lot of places I would go to before I would go to Haiti, and-- "

"Doc, we are running at little late," I said, glancing at my watch to show I wasn't making it up. He got the message. He jumped out of the little swivel stool that was backed into the corner and said he would be right back.

He quickly returned with a list in hand. His head was down and he was shaking it disapprovingly. "OK," he breathed. "First of all you need to take a sequence of Malarone pills," he said, handing me two prescriptions. "This will help protect you against malaria. You should know this does not absolutely eliminate the risk, but if you follow the instructions, your chances of contracting malaria will be significantly reduced."

"What instructions?"

"You need to take a dose for four days before you arrive in Haiti, then take a dose every day you are there and then for five days after you return. If you don't follow these instructions the medication will not work," he said, adding: "By the way, these pills make most people sick, with some people reacting as if they have the flu." He seemed to enjoy the idea there was going to be some discomfort associated with our trip preparation.

"You will also need injections for Hepatitis A, typhoid, polio, yellow fever, Hepatitis B, rabies, MMR and Tetanus -- all of which we can do for you this afternoon. We have designed immunization packages for the various Third World countries. I can have a nurse in here as soon as one is available." The smirk on his face demonstrated he felt validated in his view going to Haiti was a dumb idea.

In the meantime, Kathi was doing a little quick math, adding up the number of the shots he had just described. Kathi is petrified of needles, nearly always passing out when she receives an injection. In the event of multiple injections, passing out was a certainty. I had lost count of the number of shots he had just rattled off, but it sure seemed like a lot. Kathi already had "that look" on her face and the needles hadn't even been loaded onto the nurse's tray. Seeing Kathi in anguish, the doctor viewed this as an opening to make one last-ditch effort to try and dissuade us -- or at least, discourage my ghost-white wife. Taking a very authoritative tone, he asked: "Are you sure you want to go through with all of this?"

"Of course we do!" I blurted, before Kathi had a chance to respond. She was wilting before our eyes, unable to string together any kind of answer, so my declaration hung there, uncontested. The doctor exited the room with a "you'll-be-sorry" look on his face, leaving us to wait it out until a nurse with the tray of

operate with impunity in the capital of Port-Au-Prince. Targets for kidnapping for ransom include wealthy Haitians, as well as foreign aid workers, even diplomats."

Rick never mentioned anything about a U.N. stabilization force.

"This travel warning is being issued to warn all American citizens of the continued dangers of traveling to Haiti. The severity is very high."

I sat back and stared at my computer screen. None of this was very encouraging; especially the 'severity is very high' part. I read the whole page again, and the news didn't get any better the second time around.

This was unexpected.

My first reaction was to go into denial. I figured the embassy was just covering its rear, telling myself it probably issues these kinds of statements all the time. I told myself not to overreact to this kind of bureaucratic statement. Besides, Rick had said nothing about any of this, and he and Peggy had safely made a number of trips to Haiti.

I went back to the directory page that lists every country. Only three had red travel-warning icons underneath their listing. Haiti was one of them. My CYA theory was crumbling like a three-day-old oatmeal cookie. Kathi was right; I hadn't really thought all of this through.

I stared out the window and wondered what would be the best way to tell Kathi about this new information. When should I tell her? She had suffered through a rough day. I didn't know what she would take as worse news -- the fact that there was a severe travel warning for Haiti, or that she may have just taken a fistful of needles for nothing.

I thought I better have some real hard back up data before I shared the news with my wife. I really wasn't prepared the other night at dinner and things got off to an awful start. Kathi is analytical and needs to know the facts. My best bet was to go back to the source. I picked up the phone and called Rick.

He answered right away and we exchanged pleasantries. He was excited to hear the news we were thinking of going to Haiti. Then he confirmed that, yes, Haiti had become more dangerous in recent months. The country really hadn't had its own government in the last couple of years and elections had kept getting postponed. He gave me Father Tom's e-mail address and recommended I ask him. "Father Tom is a straight shooter," Rick said. "He'll tell you what's happening there, and for the record, I would believe him before I would believe anything the embassy is saying."

I started typing as soon as the headset hit the cradle. I wrote from the heart, telling Father Tom how profoundly impressed I was by what he was doing and how I wanted to meet him, simply because I believed I would be a better man for doing so. I also told him that Kathi and I were planning a trip, but had concerns about our safety due to a travel warning. I wouldn't make any further plans until I heard back from him. After I was done, I headed off to bed, deciding not to say anything about the travel warnings to Kathi that night.

There also was something else I wanted to talk about with Kathi, something much more substantial than our travel plans. I was going to need the right time and place to begin that discussion. I assumed Father Tom would substantiate the travel warning, and then I could tell her I thought it would be best to postpone our trip. And, maybe while I was at it, I could talk to her about something else that was rattling around in my mind.

Father Tom responded by the following morning. He thanked me for my comments and he said he was looking forward to meeting me. Someday, he would love to show me around. But that someday would not be anytime soon. He advised us to postpone our trip. The conditions were very bad and the travel warning was accurate. While I was reading his email, Kathi knocked on the door and asked if I needed a refill on my coffee. "Come in, baby," I said, "there's something I need to talk to you about."

I started the conversation by telling her about the travel warning, and that Father Tom had confirmed it. I told her I still wanted to go to Haiti, but the trip was going to be postponed for a while. Surprisingly, she was unfazed, even relieved, by this news. She bounced up from the chair ready to get on with the rest of her day. She didn't even express any resentment about the premature immunization package.

"Honey, before you go, there is something else I want to talk to you about."

"Sure, what?"

"What would you say if I said I might want to adopt a couple of kids?"

Blank stare. "You hate kids."

Pause. "Hate is the wrong word. I don't hate them."

"Sure you do. And, I have a zillion examples. Where should I start? How about the fact that I've always wanted to go to Disneyland with you, but you won't go there because you are afraid that kids will be there. Or, how about, every time we are in a restaurant with screaming kids you throw your own tantrum about their behavior. And besides, you had the medical procedure proving that you *do* hate kids."

"That was a long time ago, too long ago to prove anything."

"Last Friday at Capital Grille was not a long time ago."

"I was talking about the vasectomy, and, for the record, my reaction last Friday night was not out of line. Capital Grille is not a family restaurant, so those kids should not have been there in the first place. And besides those parents were irresponsible by not managing their kids. Everyone else was annoyed too. And one more thing, if we did have kids, they would never be running around raising hell in a nice restaurant."

She was scrunching her nose again, a facial feature that was becoming all too familiar.

"Craig, let's back up. What has been in your cereal lately? There is something seriously out of whack with you. A few nights ago you tell me you want to go to Haiti, and the only reason I can figure out why is because your golf buddy did. Now, you are telling me you want to adopt a couple of kids. What has gotten into you? And before you answer, no, I am not interested in adopting kids even though I would love to. I know it is not right for you."

"How do you know that?"

"Because I know you and I love you. You and kids are not compatible. Honey, you are 51 years old, and there has not been one day in your life that you wanted kids.

You can't survive Thanksgiving dinner with our nieces and nephews. Now you are saying you want your own kids?"

"Maybe."

"Sweetie, just because you are attracted to the nobility of adopting kids from a Third World country doesn't mean it is the right thing for us to do. Rick and Peggy are better -- let me rephrase that -- different people than us. Their adopting doesn't mean it is right for you ... or us."

"Kath, I am not suggesting we do this only because someone else did it. Don't you see how it would be a tangible way to give something back ... OK. Let's say I suck it up and we adopt a couple of kids. We would literally be saving their lives! Let me ask you a question. If you were walking down the street, and you heard a child's voice calling out for help from a burning building, would you run in there to try to save them?"

"Of course I would."

"Honey, Haiti is a burning building and the flames are out of control."

"Craiger, you are too ... too ...," she stopped in the middle of her sentence. She sat down. She looked like she was about to cry. There was a long pause and she took a sip of her coffee, then an extra large deep breath. She put her coffee down, and started fluffing her hair, something she does when I am frustrating her. I had introduced an idea that offered her something she had always wanted, but couldn't have. I understood why she was frustrated. She knew all too well the reasons why this was a great idea and a very bad idea all at the same time. I had taken her to an emotional boiling point, and stacked on top of the experience with the immunization package, she had

had enough of Haiti and me.

She said she had some stuff to do, and staggered out of my office. As she was walking down the hall I added, "Hey, hon, it's just an idea. We have plenty of time to kick it around. I just thought it was a possibility we should talk about. That's all. I haven't even decided that I would … I mean … I would have …" And then I stopped, realizing she was long gone and I was just muttering to myself.

I was deflated. This whole thing, Haiti, adopting kids, and the pending new lease on life sat at a tipping point. My emotional high had been brought back to earth, trumped by the gangs of Port-Au-Prince. But it wasn't just the violence in Haiti. My extremely practical wife had reminded me about the realities that have segregated kids and me. It seemed to me, as far as she was concerned, any further discussion on the subject was simply perpetuating a ridiculous idea. This whole thing could have easily died and been buried under the pile of the other ideas that, for whatever reason, we never followed through on.

Except for one thing. I decided to take Kathi skiing.

# Chapter 5

## Foreign Soil

We were leaving in a week. I had reserved a lodge suite at one of Kathi's favorite places to ski in the world. I figured I owed her one. My emotions, combined with my boredom, had gotten the better of me and I had jumped the gun with my idea about the trip to Haiti. In retrospect, I should have approached it all a little more deliberately, and I felt bad about putting Kathi through unnecessary stress.

Even though Kathi had kiboshed my idea of adopting a couple of kids from Haiti, the little sneak had gone off and quietly conducted a little research on her own. She had found a number of international adoption organizations and agencies specializing in adoptions from Haiti. One night without saying anything she had left a small stack of write-ups about the various organizations on my desk. She had drawn a star on one of the pages, and she had printed across the top of it, THIS ONE LOOKS GOOD. It was an organization that promoted Haiti adoptions, and amazingly enough, it was located 45 minutes from where we were skiing.

I didn't say anything about it for a few days, and neither did she. And then on the spur of the moment during dinner I asked her, "So, did you change your mind?"

"About what?"

"Did you change your mind about me and fatherhood?"

She started to grin, which I found more appealing than the scrunched-up nose.

"I was wondering when you were going to say something. I put that stuff on your desk just for the heck of it. I thought about it a little more and I would love to adopt a couple of kids, and there are millions of orphans in this world who need a home. I'm just worried about you."

"Honey, I have been successful in most of the things I have done so far in my life. If I decided that I wanted to be a father, I would be a very good one."

"I believe that, Craiger. Here's what I can't let go of. We have the time and the resources to do this. What better thing could we be doing than to contribute something for the rest our lives? There are millions of kids in desperate places who need a home, a big part of me says it would be a shame if we didn't do this."

"And what does the other part say?"

"Honey, I say we don't need to make any decisions now. Let's keep thinking about it for a while. I do think it is a weird coincidence that you decide to take us skiing here, and at the same time, I find an organization nearby that is involved in Haiti."

We had found a peaceful middle ground, and agreed to keep the possibilities that were in front of us alive. We found it easy to be consumed by something we didn't understand. I told her that I would call the adoption organization in the morning. I wanted to hear what they had to say.

It was good to get away for a mini-vacation, and the skiing was great. The agency had invited us down to visit and after three straight days of skiing we needed a morning off. George and Mark, the directors, were gracious and informative. They had overseen the construction of an orphanage in a small village outside Port-Au-Prince. The building could house up to 50 children, and they had just begun the process of having children adopted. They experienced plenty of challenges working in Haiti, and because of the recent heightened dangers, they hadn't been there for more than a year. They felt guilty about that. They advised us not to go now, but as soon as it was safe, they would love to have us go down with them.

We were both impressed with their candor and sincerity. They were cardigan sweater types and Kathi thought that they were "sweet." I saw them as the kind of people you would want as your neighbors. They were very different from the executives I use to interface with and I imagined that in a business sense, they might have been a little naïve. Our time spent with them was very valuable -- the encounter was our first look at what was involved in adopting children from Haiti.

We thanked them for giving us the overview. As Mark

and George walked us to the door, they stopped in the lobby to show us pictures of the orphanage and the children. The dozens of pictures we saw reinforced a sentiment that had been brewing inside of me since my discussion with Rick on the 10th fairway. The magic in the children's eyes and the brilliance of their smiles fueled my desire to experience Haiti. Kathi was so emotionally captivated by the pictures that she started to tear up. I nearly joined her.

As we went to shake hands, I asked, "How do you pay for all of this?"

Both of their heads dropped, and Mark started to rock from side to side. He stammered out a reply. "We have survived on private donations, and the truth of the matter is, things on that front have dried up a little bit."

In a nanosecond Kathi jumped into the conversation "Maybe we could help out. We love to give to organizations that are doing something worthwhile." She looked up at me expecting back up.

"We might be interested in making a contribution," I said in a more cautious tone. "I would need to see some documentation and your tax returns, but I see this as something we might want to contribute to." My Good Samaritan wife wrapped her arms around me approvingly. It was time to go. We all shook hands and said we would keep in touch.

A few weeks went by and we corresponded back and forth with Mark. Kathi and I ended up making a donation, stating we would track the progress of the organization. If we saw a reasonable level of productivity, we would consider adding to that contribution. The more we considered it the more interested we became in the possibility of adopting a couple of kids from Haiti. Although we were a long way from making a definitive decision one way or another, there were some powerful forces tugging at us and we decided to start the very first phase of the adoption process called a home study. It didn't hurt to get the ball rolling. Initiating the formal process allowed us to keep our options open if and when we decided to follow through on what was at times a very compelling idea.

* * *

About six weeks after our first meeting, Mark and I decided to go to Haiti. The dangers in Haiti had subsided only a little, but we had decided the situation was as good as it was going to get. Mark hadn't visited the orphanage in more than 14 months, and he was eager to check in. My sense of adventure was kicking in, and since my recent donation had given me some skin in the game, I wanted to see how my money was being spent. Besides, going to Haiti with someone who had experience traveling through the country made much more sense than going on my own.

However, it didn't make sense to have Kathi join us. Our research had shown that the rash of kidnappings had slowed down, but there were still some considerable risks, and I did not want to subject Kathi to those risks. She made me promise two things to her before I left. One, I would do everything possible while I was there to ensure my safety and, two, I wouldn't fall in love with any kids and bring them home.

* * *

The guess I had given Kathi turned out to be correct. Port-Au-Prince is only an hour and a half flight from Miami. As we approached Haiti, it looked like any other Caribbean island. I would soon discover that the view from 30,000 feet is a great neutralizer. We landed on a tarmac of cracked asphalt and protruding weeds. There was a steel drum band outside of the terminal that served as the welcoming committee. Musical capabilities aside, the five-piece band brought a certain charm to a moment in which my anxiety was starting to percolate.

The sense of charm quickly left me once I entered the commotion-filled terminal. There was an over-abundance of yelling and pointing, with bodies darting and shifting at a rapid pace. It didn't appear anyone was in charge of the place, or if there was, they were on a break. Chaotic energy filled the steamy building as we waited for our bags. I hadn't brought much for me, but I had packed my weight limit in toys, clothes, and candy for the orphanage.

Two men who worked for the orphanage greeted us. The first was Antoine, our driver, and the second gave us his name and shook our hands. I hadn't understood him, which I took as a red flag when I learned he was to be our interpreter. Whatever his name was, he didn't have much to do as we scrambled around looking for our bags. We left the airport compound and started the drive out to the village of Lamardelle. I asked how far we had to go and the interpreter told us "fourtie," followed by another word I didn't understand. Whether it was forty miles or forty minutes, I supposed it didn't really matter.

Given our inability to understand the interpreter, the conversation remained at a minimum. Antoine's truck was a plain gray pickup with a makeshift cage over the bed. The cage was tall and made the truck look top-heavy. The cage kept our over-stuffed luggage from spilling onto the pot-holed excuse for a road. I opened my window to get some airflow. The sights and the smells of Port-Au-Prince were living up to their billing. I had expected to witness abject poverty and so far, my expectations were being met. My first impression of Haiti was slums on steroids.

We were on a Haitian thoroughfare, a two-lane, paved road which was in need of repair. I sat and looked through the open window taking it all in. I looked down the various alleyways connecting to the main street and I saw layers of garbage that had been trampled on over time, forming a kind of urban tundra. Everything looked very unsanitary.

We approached an intersection, and the free-for-all began. There wasn't a light, sign or cop, and traffic came to a standstill, while cars and trucks jolted back and forth trying to maneuver their way out of the logjam. It was a mess, and it looked like we would be there for a while.

Antoine was a particularly aggressive driver, and he was an expert in working the horn. In a non-rhythmic, but somewhat predictable manner, he kept violently banging on the horn. From one moment to the next he stepped on the gas, then abruptly slammed on the brakes. He was sure working hard, but we weren't going anywhere. All the cars in the intersection were using this same technique, making the cars shake, instead of rolling forward. We resembled bees furiously working a honeycomb, but unlike bees, we weren't making any progress. It was a war of wills between the drivers, and Antoine had a very determined look on his face. I hadn't experienced anything like this before, but I guessed it was routine for Antoine.

The agitated intersection gave me a few minutes to remind myself of the embassy warning. As I watched vehicles try to escape the gridlock, I kept an eye out for large groups of men with guns. If anyone wanted to shoot me or kidnap me I was a sitting duck in this truck. Antoine resourcefully found a way out, quickly advancing around three other cars that had locked bumpers. We survived the intersection melee and were back on our way.

As we made our way away from town, the road deteriorated even more. It was now a combination of potholes and asphalt, with potholes holding the majority position. The streets were lined with people just watching the cars go by, a Third World parade. We abruptly turned down a small alleyway and stopped in front of what looked like a store. Without saying anything, Antoine shut off the car and got out. I asked our interpreter what was going on, and he just shrugged. It seemed to me that the orphanage wasn't getting its money's worth with the interpreter. I asked Mark and he said we were stopping to get something at the store. Mark had a knack for making guesses sound like statements of fact.

I was nervously waiting for Antoine to return for a couple of reasons. One, he was a big guy and two; he had the keys to the car. I was fixated on the front of the store; just as a dog stares out to a point of reference waiting for his master to return. Suddenly out of the front door of the unmarked store walked a big guy, with a big machine gun. I thought to myself, "This is it." I had been in Haiti less than an hour and it sure looked like there was going to be an incident. I hoped I would just be an observer, as opposed to a participant, in the event.

Antoine strutted out right behind the big guy with the gun. He had a five-gallon bottle of water slung over his shoulder. My anticipation of a gunfight was the first of a few anxiety-laced false alarms. The big guy with the machine gun turned out to be the store's security guard, something I learned from the interpreter, the first words of his I understood. The five-gallon jug was filled with drinking water for Mark and me.

We continued on through a few suburbs of Port-Au-Prince, communities that were pockets of dense population. The people had chickens, goats, and vegetables stacked on their heads as they walked around in single file looking for customers. They walked in an orderly manner, a human conveyor belt market in the streets, one with a permanent inequity of more sellers than buyers.

Mark told me we were about to turn off onto a dirt road which would take us to the orphanage. I would have described the road a bit differently. It was actually a path of rocks that, at times, did have some dirt portions. We were now in rural Haiti, and Antoine was forced to drive more slowly to maneuver around the rocks. The severity of the road was extremely hard on the tires and suspension, but it seemed like a great way for someone to keep their driving skills sharp.

We were being jostled around like a thimble in the sea, and I wondered how much farther we had to travel. Our travel conditions so far hadn't been all that comfortable and Mark's non-stop narration about what I was seeing was nothing short of aggravating. I did my best to tune him and the rocky road out, and focus on the simplicity of the life I was seeing. Some of the villagers were working in a garden or washing clothes in a small trough of water that flowed by the side of the road. Others were just standing around looking at us go by. No one seemed in much of a hurry, but they all seemed excited to see our truck approaching. Apparently, this rocky road didn't have much traffic.

Mark kept babbling and interrupting my thoughts. His observations were frequently stated as questions. "See how skinny they are?" he asked.

I didn't answer. The people I observed were thin, very thin, but I would have described them as lean, not skinny. The people of the village looked reasonably healthy and, on the whole, attractive. They had handsome features and a graceful manner about them. We arrived at a central spot in the village and Mark asked Antoine if we could pull over and stop for a few minutes. Mark wanted to give me a tour.

I saw it as a great idea. It was a chance to take a break from the rumble seat and would be my first experience of a little bit of Haiti on foot. The four of us began to walk down the narrow winding path that wove its way around stick shacks and makeshift houses. There was no electricity or fresh water. The water supply was the cement trough that ran along the side of the road. A river fed the trough, and the farther down the trough, the filthier the water. This was the community water supply. People washed clothes in it, bathed in it, brushed their teeth in it, and drank it. And so did all the farm animals.

The people in the village didn't have much. Theirs was by far the most primitive lifestyle I had ever seen. They were poor, but they weren't slobs. They took pride in keeping whatever they had clean and tidy. I saw women sweeping the dirt floors of their houses that were made out of sticks and random shapes of metal and wood. The villagers were friendly and as we walked by they said, "Bon Jour." When we made eye contact, their smiles filled me with warmth and comfort. There was a gentle, peaceful energy surrounding us as we continued to stroll along the path in the poorest country in the Western Hemisphere. The contrast with my own life back home was extreme. In Haiti I was experiencing the other end of the spectrum, a far cry from the country club brunch buffet.

We wound our way back to the main drag, but the path had taken us past our vehicle, further up the road. We were now north of our truck by a half mile. Antoine and I decided to walk back to get the truck, while Mark and the interpreter decided to wait with some villagers for us to return. As we walked, we spotted another truck that was stopped on the side of the road. There were half a dozen people milling around the truck and about a dozen pigs off to the side of the road. Antoine ran up ahead to see what the problem was. I was on my own to navigate my way past the pigs, which drifted up towards me.

The people with the truck were yelling at one another and I could see Antoine joining in the animated discussion. I guessed that the pigs had been in the truck at one point, but somehow had escaped and were enjoying a newfound sense of freedom. As I approached the pack of pigs, two of them, enjoying their freedom more than the others, began to mate. Their conduct aggravated one of the other, very big pigs, and he flew into a fit of what looked like jealous rage. That set off a violent reaction with the rest of the pigs, and a riot began to brew among them. The battle formed a barricade in the middle of the road.

As the pig fracas escalated, I was trying to find a safe way to reunite myself with Antoine, who with the others was on the opposite side of the truck from me. The pigs were dirty and dark, with very long teeth that they seemed to enjoy flashing. As they got closer, their stench slammed into me, the smell of four-day-old fish. While I was trying to recall whether I had ever heard of a pig attack on a human, Antoine was yelling and waving at me and other passengers of the truck were screaming. Panicking, Antoine began waving frantically for me to hurry up and join him. I had only one option: I was going to have to cross through the pig riot. Before I made my move, I laughed as I considered the irony of the situation -- the embassy warning had mentioned nothing about attacks by pigs. I started to make my way gingerly through the stinking, berserk mass of pigs. They squealed and snorted, so consumed with the frenzy they barely noticed me. I darted through an opening and I made my way to the other side of the pig mosh pit.

By the time I joined the others, the commotion had died down and the locals effortlessly herded the pigs back on to the truck. Antoine and I made our way back to our vehicle and were up the road picking up Mark and the interpreter in a matter of minutes. As Mark was getting into the car he asked, "What was all that noise?"

"Just some locals and a few pigs," I said.

To be honest, the walk through the village and the encounter with the pigs helped ground me in Haiti. I no longer felt like a complete stranger, and I started to relax. I stopped thinking about getting kidnapped and the dangers I had been warned about. The Haitians I had seen so far were hospitable, not hostile. Soon Mark said we were only a few minutes away from the orphanage.

I took a deep breath, and started thinking about the kids I had just seen, and the kids I was about to see at the orphanage. I thought back to my childhood, and all of the luxuries of Little League, and bicycles, and ice cream and the joy all those things had brought to me. I realized I hadn't seen much joy during my walk through the village. I also didn't remember hearing any laughter. I stared out the window and felt all kinds of sadness as I watched three barefoot kids play with a stick. They waved and smiled as we drove by. I waved back, but I couldn't return the smile. I recalled my own childhood and I knew what they were missing.

# Chapter 6

## Cartoon Walk

Haiti is hot and humid, the climate equivalent of rubbing salt into the wound of the nation's abject poverty. The streets of Port-Au-Prince emit a distinctive odor, as if everything is spoiling. The mixture of garbage heaps and oppressive heat creates a foul recipe of sickening smells. When Antoine brought the rickety truck to a stop in front of a big metal gate, the merciful flow of moving air died, and a ruthless, reeking flood of humidity permeated the cabin of the vehicle. Sweat rolled off our foreheads. The truck ride across Port-Au-Prince, the first chapter of my adventure in Haiti, was over, and a second chapter was about to begin. We had arrived at the orphanage, Enfant de Jesus.

What in the world was I doing there?

I could easily qualify as the last man you would imagine to be sitting in a truck waiting to go inside an orphanage in Haiti. In addition to not being a kid guy or a religious guy, I was not even a sympathetic guy, and visiting an orphanage in Haiti, or an orphanage anywhere, was not on the Top Ten List of Things to Do Before I Die. The question lingered in my mind without an answer. Still, there I was, on the cusp of the most radical change of my life.

During the weeks that led up to that moment, I had assumed orphanages were grim places. Children without parents carried that kind of connotation, even to an emotional hobo like me. If you were an abandoned or orphaned child, the world had dished you up a heaping spoonful of cruelty, in my view. In a perfect world, there would be no orphanages. All kids would have someone responsible to love them, hold their hands, and show them the way. Even I could see that.

So as we sat outside the gate, I braced myself for the worst. I expected to see dejected and demoralized kids longing for someone to love them. While we waited, Mark clarified the facility was actually a "crèche," not an "orphanage," and that I should use that term so I would fit in. In Haiti, crèches offer children for adoption; orphanages house and care for them until they grow into adults. To me the word "crèche" meant there were 22 kids on the other side of the gate waiting and hoping for someone to claim them.

The gate to the crèche was massive and imposing, and people on both sides milled around, waiting for someone else to open it. Fixed above us on the left side of the gate stood a tower, and in the turret of the tower I could see men with rifles. The place looked more like a concentration camp than a crèche. The gate opened and

Antoine gently stepped on the gas.

For the first time since we left Miami I heard laughter -- lots of it. Children were scattered around a play yard, and they were doing a very good job of playing -- jumping rope, kicking balls, and playing tag. Several women in the yard supervised the festivities, and they seemed to be enjoying themselves as well. We had arrived into a joyous atmosphere, and I sensed a sparkling and effervescent energy missing from my earlier observations of Haiti. This place looked fun, and if the children here were orphans, they didn't seem to be all that upset about it.

Beyond the playful laughter was a massive gray concrete structure. The building looked like a small military fortress; solid, rugged, with crisply-defined lines. Its architecture contrasted sharply with the stick shacks I had seen during my trip through the village. The unpainted structure sat as a pillar of strength behind the children jumping rope and playing ball. It was there to protect those who lived inside it. The guards in the tower -- who hadn't taken their eyes off me since I had arrived -- served as a punctuation mark to the building's statement of protective fortitude.

I stepped out of the truck and stood there, looking around. The play yard resembled a scene from a neighborhood park on a Saturday afternoon, a comforting departure from my expectations. The kids seemed to be having a great time and I was beginning to enjoy being there. The joyous laughter erased my anxiety about the poverty-stricken, heat and humidity-soaked scenery I had just hurtled through. I even began to forget my scrape with the crazed pigs. I became captivated with the much happier scene that unfolded before me. The 20 or so laughing, playing children gave off a genuine mood of innocence and charm. I had always been skeptical of people who claimed a specific moment changed them, but as I stood there I could feel myself crossing a border, transforming into a "kid guy."

Looming over the playful scene was the hard fact that if the kids had not been in the crèche, they very likely would have died. According to the UN Children's Fund, children born in Haiti are more likely to die in early childhood than in any other country in the Western Hemisphere. But inside these protective walls were kids full of life. Their energy brought a rush of memories about my childhood and how playing was such a part of it. I also thought about how good I had had it for the past 51 years. I considered all of the grand possibilities that had come my way, provided by loving parents, great friends, and the moments that had formed my life. I wondered what lay in store for the kids in the crèche ... What was their destiny, and who, if anyone, would help shape their futures?

My thoughts were interrupted by a woman who walked up to me and enthusiastically extended her hand. "Hello Craig, I'm Gina."

Gina Ferrus Duncan was born in Haiti in 1960 in a small province on the southeast coast called Petit-Goave. One of eight children and the only one born in a hospital, Gina and her family moved to Brooklyn, N.Y. when she was four. When Gina was a teenager, her family moved to Montreal and her parents purchased a 60-bed nursing home in Quebec. This was a time of discovery for Gina as she worked side by side with her parents in the nursing home. The experience gave her a broader perspective on the human condition and what it meant to care for others.

After graduating from high school Gina made the first of many trips back to Haiti. Those first trips were filled with shock and disappointment as she saw how things had deteriorated in her native country. The beautiful Haiti of her memories lay in ruins. She made frequent trips between Haiti and North America while she pursued her advanced degrees. Her first job after school was in a burn unit at Montreal's General Hospital. But she knew that job would be only temporary, as she felt drawn to return and try to make a difference in her homeland.

She moved back to Haiti and married Lucien Duncan. Gina went to work for the hospital in Port-Au-Prince and began to witness a disturbing lack of general health care for the children of Haiti. She saw children left to die painful deaths. Gina began to visit local orphanages in search of solutions. One day a man came to her carrying an infant. He had found twin girls in a garbage pile -- one was dead, but the other clung to life. She adopted the baby and named her Sarah. That is how the mission of saving Haiti's children began for Gina and Lucien.

Construction for Enfant de Jesus began in 2003. Over the next year and a half over 400 Haitian and American volunteers worked on the 14,000-square foot building and the wall that encloses the four-acre compound. All who participated endured the demanding rigors of a construction project in a Third World country. The operative description of the task was perseverance; from start to finish nothing came easy. In May 2004 the building was completed and 150 people attended a ceremony to mark the official opening of the crèche. The facility sits on the Duncan family plantation in the rural village of Lamardelle. The building stands as an impressive achievement of the human spirit, and all who participated in its construction can be proud.

Gina is a perfectionist, something that was clear to me after she invited me on a tour of the place. What I saw surpassed my expectations. The facility was immaculate; the tile floors were sparkling clean. There was a comforting hint of antiseptic in the air. The building had three wings and a big main area where the kids ate. There was a preschool, a big kitchen and a laundry area. The staff wore uniforms and were diligently focused on their tasks. Dinner was being prepared and the kitchen was in line with everything else -- spotless and orderly. The tables were set and the place looked crisp and organized. It was remarkable to see such a methodical and systematic setting; especially after all of the chaos and poverty I had witnessed since I got off the airplane.

Gina's standards were high and the staff was committed to excellence. The entire place, the building, the people, the cleanliness, the order -- all seemed out of place in Haiti. I was very impressed, and at the same time, very relieved. My preconceptions had made me dread what I would find behind the walls of the crèche, but after the tour I could barely contain my enthusiasm. I was so thrilled I was going to get to stay here, instead of some of the other places I had seen along the way. I wanted to celebrate and I knew just the place: The play yard where I had first seen the 20 or so kids. Contrary to what many believe about me, I have a playful side, and instinct compelled me to go out and join in the fun.

Back at home the first thing Kathi and I would do in the morning was walk the dogs. We'd go out at the crack of dawn before anyone else was up in the neighborhood. It was a time for us to hold hands before the day began and preoccupations got in the way. I don't tell people this, but sometimes when I was in a very playful mood, I would walk ahead of her holding both of the dog's leashes and strut in a goofy walk inspired by a cartoon character I remembered from when I was kid. It was a silly thing to do, but on the other hand, it was kind of fun. Kathi patronized me with nervous laughter, mortified that one of the neighbors might see me and conclude I had lost my senses. I didn't do it very often, because the walk had to coincide with a certain mood, but my cartoon-like walk is one of the precious little secrets I share with my mate. It is one of the hundreds of intimate fibers that connect me to her, and it represents a bit of the magic in our relationship.

The silly walk rushed to my mind because of something that happened right after Gina wrapped up the tour. A staff member signaled to Gina, indicating she needed a minute with her. I politely excused myself, and I began to retrace my steps back to the play yard. As I approached the door to the outside, I noticed a little girl in the corner by the kitchen, kneeling down to tie her shoes. In the quiet of the moment I took a long look at her. She was dainty and stunningly beautiful, like a four-year-old version of Diana Ross, with high cheek bones and saucer-sized eyes. She neatly wore a red dress with matching red socks and clean white shoes. Like the other children she was perfectly groomed, as if she were on her way to Sunday school. She looked at me with soulful eyes that invited me toward her. When she finished tying her shoes, she jumped up and walked over to meet me.

As we began to walk to the door together, she reached out to grab my hand, and as our hands clasped she did something incredible and unforgettable. She stopped walking normally. She threw her legs out in front her in an exaggerated fashion and comically swayed back and forth in the same cartoon-like manner I did on some mornings with Kathi. It was as if she had seen me do the walk before and she was mimicking the way I did it. No one other than Kathi had ever seen my goofy little walk, but somehow this little girl in a red dress with matching socks knew it, or at least a hauntingly similar version of it. I was stunned. It was all I could do to keep my legs moving to keep up with her. Even though I was seeing it, I still couldn't believe it.

I asked myself, "This didn't just happen, did it?" Although I knew the idea was crazy, I felt it had to be something more than an uncanny coincidence. I have a hard time buying such things, but I began asking myself, "Was this some sort of sign?"

She continued her animated walk, smiling up at me now and again. I just stumbled along until we got to the door. We stepped outside into the piercing sunlight and she looked up at me with her soulful eyes, squeezing my hand as if she was trying to tell me something. Then she let go of my hand and ran away to join her friends in the yard. She suddenly glanced back at me one more time and gently smiled, looking as if she knew what had just crossed my mind. At that instant my trip took on a whole new meaning.

Her name was Esperancia, which means hope. Gina

told me she was four years old. Gina and Lucien had found her in a mountainside village when she was about two. She was so skinny and malnourished she was little more than skin and bones. Her mother had had seven or eight children from various fathers, all of whom had come and gone, and she had no means to take care of the little ones. Esperancia was one of the lucky ones because she had been taken away to live in the crèche, where she had been living for nearly two years the day I met her. During that time no one had stepped forward to adopt her, which was amazing to me. She was a beautiful little girl, full of charisma and charm. I thought about some of the things she could be doing if she lived in the U.S. Who knows what she could become given the right set of circumstances?

I played with the children in the yard for about an hour or so. In many ways it was a celebration; we played ball and tag, and I even tried to teach a couple of the kids how to throw a Frisbee. Esperancia and I would occasionally glance over at each other, and when our eyes made contact, she smiled at me. At various times all the kids came up to say hi and to check me out. It was fun to meet them and to try and understand their names. The crèche hadn't had many visitors in the last year and I was a new point of interest.

At last the kids received a signal from one of the staff -- they called them "Aunties" -- and they quickly formed a line and marched in to the main area singing a song as dinner was served. For a big group of little kids, they were remarkably well-behaved. The dinner was a healthy helping of rice and beans with plantains on the side.

I had promised Kathi I would let her know as soon as I

could that I had arrived safely. I found a towel from one of the bathrooms and wiped off the sweat I had worked up running around the yard with the kids. It seemed like a perfect time for me to write her a cyber note.

*kathi, the children are eating dinner and I have a minute to write you - sorry this won't be much but Mark also wants to use the computer to check in with his family - I can't tell you how much I would rather be talking to you but this e-mail will have to do- the first thing that comes to my mind is how disappointed I am that you are not here to share this experience with me... but it has been an unbelievable day...first of all I am safe and we made it out to the orphanage without incident...although I thought all hell was going to break loose a couple of times along the way- the orphanage is exceeding any expectations that I had...very clean...extremely well run by a great staff... ...and the kids...holy cow!*

*They are all very loveable... very affectionate and playful- I have already connected with one young girl and I have to tell you the story- you are not going to believe this but I am not exaggerating- this happened exactly as I will tell you- I had only been here a short while and I was walking out to the yard when one of the little girls (her name is esperancia) came over to walk with me and when she did she started walking in that way I sometimes walk in the morning with the dogs...I was blown away.....it was almost spooky!*

*I emotionally red-lined more than once today and many times today I felt like crying and other times I was laughing hysterically- I took some pictures but got so carried away with playing with them that the picture taking took a back seat- the drive out here was awful because of what I saw but once we got here I found a little piece of magic. Gina is terrific and her staff is excellent- this is an orphanage that sets a high standard – I can't tell you how disappointed I am that you are not here-- I don't want to jump the gun , and I know we said that I would not identify any kids for us to adopt unless something unique came up...but.....I don't know if I have seen anything more unique.... i mean she did the walk, just like me..... can you be thinking what I am thinking.... I have to wonder if esperancia is supposed to be our daughter - I love you I will write you tomorrow as soon as I can get back on the computer – craig.*

Soon it was bedtime for the kids and, in line with everything else I had seen in the crèche, the process of getting ready for bed was handled in a very orderly manner. I meandered through the sleeping quarters saying good night to the children. These 22 kids were some of the lucky ones. They had been given up or abandoned, but that night they were not alone. They all looked so healthy and I could see from just the few hours I had been there how much effort went into caring for them. I assumed that someday most of them would have a home to go to. On that same night as I watched the Aunties tuck in the children, there were plenty of other orphaned kids in Haiti who were still wandering around, scrounging for something to eat and searching for a safe place to lie down.

I arrived at Esperancia's bed and she was almost asleep. She rolled over and we stared at each other as if we were both trying to solve some sort of puzzle. I whispered "Good night, sweetheart" and in perfect English she said, "Good night," then rolled over and went to sleep.

It was time for me to do the same. I have had many good days in my lifetime, and as this day was coming to an end, I would count it as one of them.

# Chapter 7

## Photo Opportunity

There were 22 kids in the crèche. Exactly half of them had been matched with a family and were waiting for paperwork to be completed so they could go to their new home. The remaining children were unclaimed, still waiting for someone to adopt them. Many international adoptions begin in cyberspace, on the web page of an adoption organization. Couples in the market to adopt a child shop around, for lack of a better term, looking at pictures on various sites to see if they might connect with a child through his or her image. In some countries, the process is even more random, with adoptive families given a number matched to an orphaned child. In cases like this, a family will travel to a country to pick up a child whom they have never even seen a picture of.

All countries have differences in their adoption

process, but the core of the system is very similar. International adoption requires money and patience. An international adoption can cost $25,000 or more for one child and the process can take up to 18 to 24 months -- or even longer -- to complete. In 2006, about 20,679 international adoptions were completed to the U.S., according to the State Department. If that many children went to American families that year, it surprised me that any of the 11 unchosen kids at the crèche were still available for adoption. It broke my heart that half of the kids did not have a family to go to soon. They looked like great kids, and that especially rang true for Esperancia, who was one of the most charming kids in the facility.

Gina carried out a tradition in the crèche once a child had been matched with a family: She placed pictures of the adoptive family around the child's bed. While it was a sweet thing to do for the kid who was matched, it created a haves- and haves-not situation in the facility. The children with no pictures were like the kids left on the playground after all the teams have chosen members. Adding to the heartbreak of not having a family was the knowledge that some of their friends had been chosen instead of them.

When I woke up on my first morning in the crèche, I went to look at the pictures on the walls of the children's bedroom. The room was empty as the kids had already started their day. Since I didn't know which bed was whose, and since I didn't know the kids very well, I couldn't identify which kids had pictures and which didn't. I decided to try and guess who had been matched with families by following the kids, examining facial expressions and watching body language. It was an interesting exercise for me while I was hanging out.

One of the real stars of the orphanage was a boy named Amelec. His body language conveyed confidence and positive energy. It was a safe bet he had been matched with a family the minute his picture hit the web. He had an infectious laugh, seemed very bright, and was the leader of the pack. His charismatic personality contributed to making the crèche a happy place. I was sure there were photos of a family over his bed. I gazed around at some of the other children, which was enjoyable to do -- a great way to start the day. As with so many kids, it was easy to see their distinctive personalities and energies while they interacted and played. Gina said that breakfast would be served in a few minutes, and she asked if I would join her. I made mental notes on which kids I guessed had been matched with a family, and which hadn't. While I could, I slipped away for a minute to see if Kathi had responded to the e-mail I sent her last night.

*Craig, Oh my gosh….you can't believe how excited I was to get your e-mail. Honey I was ecstatic reading it. First of all I am glad you are safe and I too am disappointed that I am not with you sharing this experience…and to think that little girl did the fancy walk, maybe she has been waiting for you, I will totally trust your decision so if she is the one, I am thrilled. How do you communicate with them? Oh my gosh, I have so many questions……..*

I took a deep breath, signed off from email, and got up to wash my hands for breakfast. Kathi's e-mail confirmed what I had been thinking about during a restless night.

As long as it was OK with Gina, Esperancia was going to become our daughter. I figured the next step was to learn what we had to do procedurally to commit to our desire to adopt her. Surprisingly, for a guy who swore he would never be a dad, the decision to adopt Esperancia seemed very natural and easy. I began to convince myself that at 51, it was time. More importantly I felt connected to Esperancia in some way.

During breakfast I asked Gina if Kathi and I could begin the process of adopting Esperancia.

Gina was ecstatic, saying, "Craig, I saw the connection between you two right off the bat."

The transformation was complete -- I had become a kid guy.

But an instant later I found myself thinking about jumping back to the other side of the line. The safe side. As the conversation went on my feet started to get cold, probably because there was so much about all of this that I didn't know or understand. Even though adopting Esperancia felt very natural, now that I was pulling the trigger I felt a little out of control. What if I was wrong? What if I could not do this? Whenever I start feeling out of control, I always try to buy some time.

I asked Gina for a couple of day's grace period, just in case I changed my mind. The minute I made the suggestion I felt foolish. How could I whipsaw through a decision as important as this? Based on the proposition -- committing to a child for life -- asking for a couple days' grace period before I could say I was absolutely sure may have been logical -- or it may have been selfish. In any case it put a big damper on the euphoria of the moment.

If I thought about it, I probably could have come up

with a million reasons not to adopt Esperancia, but they would all be trumped by an irrefutable fact. Adopting her was the right thing to do. But … I just wanted to leave the back door a little bit ajar if I woke up in a cold sweat sometime over the next two days. Nonetheless, I quickly reassured Gina I wasn't trying to back out. "I just want to sleep on it a night or two, even though it sure seems like the right thing to do," I told her.

The uncertainty I had created took center stage, and although Gina was very understanding, I know she was a little disappointed I had put an asterisk next to the statement she had been waiting two years to hear. She obviously felt Esperancia was a very special child and it was frustrating that no one had wanted to adopt her. And now she was probably questioning my sincerity even though I awkwardly loaded the rest of the conversation with comments about "how excited Kathi and I were" and "what a great kid Esperancia is." In the process of trying to recover from bursting Gina's balloon, I never got around to asking her which kids were matched with families and which were still available. That would have to come later.

Even though I had given myself an out, deep down I could feel that things were in motion, and Kathi and I were going to adopt Esperancia. I was on my way to fatherhood. During the next few days Esperancia and I were like peas and carrots. I went to her preschool class, watched her run around with the others in the yard, and even sat next to her one night at dinner. Obviously this was not customary for one of the grownups to eat at one of the kids' tables, but it was fun for me. I was really impressed with the children's manners and their eating etiquette. They were very polite and well-behaved during the meal. Their manners were a credit to those who managed and worked at the crèche.

When Esperancia and I weren't hanging out, Amelec and I began to chum around. He was really fun to be around, as he had near-magical charisma and loved to play ball. He was very athletic, and the more I saw him in action the more I believed he was the alpha male of the group of boys. It struck me he was one of the happiest little boys I had ever seen.

Esperancia was also making a powerful impression on me. I noticed many things about her that made her unique. One morning as I wandered the halls while the children were outside playing, I saw her inside by herself straightening her bed. She did not see me, but I could see she took great pride in her surroundings, another example of why she would be a great addition to a family. No cold sweats visited me the next few nights. In fact, as time passed, I became more certain I was ready.

The next day I cut the cord on the safety net and told Gina it was official. Kathi and I were all in. We wanted to adopt Esperancia.

Gina simply replied, "I knew it! I knew this was going to happen all along. I could see it, Craig -- this is what I do. You and Esperancia are meant to be together -- she will be a great daughter for you." We sat down on a bench and our conversation drifted into the specifics of starting the adoption process. Right then Amelec ran by, smiling, laughing, and having a grand time as he always seemed to be. My curiosity got the better of me: I interrupted Gina's description of what it would take for us to adopt Esperancia, and asked her about Amelec's future home and the lucky family who had chosen him long ago.

Gina sighed and shook her head. She glanced at Amelec, who tore across the play field, a broad grin sprawling across his face. "He has no home, not yet," she said sadly. "We are still patiently waiting for someone to take him."

I was floored. I felt that all 11 of the unclaimed children in the crèche were great kids, and would be wonderful additions to any family. But Amelec seemed to me a standout, and it didn't make any sense to me that he was still waiting.

"Why not?" I asked Gina, so taken aback I almost asked whether she was joking.

"I think it is because Amelec's picture on the web site is not very good."

"That's it? One bad picture?"

Before I could ask why they did not just take another picture, Gina shook her head and shrugged her shoulders, looking as if she were going to cry. She took the adoption of these kids personally. She told me as far as she knew no one had even inquired about Amelec. I viewed it as a tragedy. Because of poor marketing -- a single picture that did not make the boy look attractive enough -- Amelec had been passed over by families looking to adopt. The tragedy was further compounded by my experience of him the last few days. I had gotten to know Amelec a little and I believed he would make a great son who would grow into a distinctive person.

As I stared off into the play yard to watch him run around with his friends, I asked myself whether my encounter with Amelec could be more than just a coincidence of timing. I had just committed myself to become Esperancia's father and was excited about what that would bring. At that point there was no looking back; I felt good about the decision to adopt Esperancia. But in the same moment, I had discovered a special young boy who was in the market for a dad, which, as of a few minutes earlier, is what I was becoming.

I wondered how this string of events was continuing to happen ... the dots seemed to be connecting themselves. Kathi and I had talked about adopting a boy his age, and Amelec's profile was exactly what we had discussed in our many conversations. I closed my eyes and I could already see us playing catch together. We had another empty bedroom in the house which would be perfect for him. Was this another "meant to be" kind of thing? Amelec seemed like such a wonderful kid and I knew we could give him a wonderful home ... but I had just committed to adopting Esperancia... but now I had the opportunity to double down .. but ...

BUT ...

My mind was racing. Gina sat with me quietly. She seemed to know what I was thinking. Before I spoke I cautioned myself to make sure I was not just getting caught up in the emotion of the moment. I did not want to start something, then put it on hold like I had done the other day, looking like a schizophrenic. Also, Kathi had not met either child. Although they both seemed to be extraordinary kids, and I could see how the four of us would make a great family, should I really be making this decision by myself? On the other hand, life is imperfect, and some of the most beautiful pieces of life do not fall into neat and orderly rows. Just being here was a good reminder of that. The only thing that made the moment not "perfect" was that Kathi was not there. Other than that, there was a lot of perfect right there in front of me, and Amelec seemed like a perfect match for our family. His unattractive photo on a web page offered me an opportunity I could not pass up.

Gina and I had been sitting in silence from the moment she welled up at the thought of Amelec's unfortunate photograph. I glanced at her, then stared her right in the eye. She stared back. After a moment, I broke the silence.

"Gina, as of now, Amelec has a family. If it is okay with you, Kathi and I will be his parents. Esperancia now has a brother. And Amelec has a sister."

Gina's face broke into a soft smile. She rose from the bench and I did the same. This time there was no babbling about sleeping on it, or any other caveats. She wrapped her arms around me and said, "Thank you, thank you. It has been so heartbreaking to see Amelec get passed over." She began to cry again. "Amelec will be a great son for you."

She grabbed both of my hands. "You will be a great father, Craig. You should know what a noble and gracious thing you are doing."

I was speechless. It had all happened so quickly. I now had a daughter, and a son, and I was certain that I had no idea what I was getting myself into. It was just something I wanted to do. And I was certain it was also the right thing to do.

The moment and all of its meaning hit me, and it was my turn to tear up. I returned Gina's hug and there was nothing more to say. We hugged for a long time... in magnificent silence. When the embrace stopped I wiped the tears from my face. I nodded in silence, as if to let Gina know everything was going to be OK. Then I headed straight for the computer. I had some explaining to do.

*kathi- I spoke to gina this morning and you have a daughter. gina was thrilled with our decision and we will tell esperancia that I am going to be her dad sometime before I leave- I also have some other news, we also have a son- remember that kid amelec who I was telling you about- remember I described him as the pick of the litter (probably don't want to repeat that phrase to our friends). well I was shocked but gina told me this morning he is available- apparently he has a horrible picture on the web page and no one has taken him- first of all I can't believe they have a bad picture of this kid on the web page but somehow it means he can be our son- you will love this kid- he is stocky- athletic and a winner- he has a face full of energy and emotion - kinda looks like the quarterback who plays for the jacksonville jags- he has a huge heart and he and I get along great-now if you are really adamant and you need some time about this we can find a way to put this on hold but I think you are just going to have to trust me on this one- how about that- we have two kids- and by the way, two great kids- we will give them all of the love that anyone can- I am very excited and wish you were here to share in all of this first hand- I love you and you will be the best mom any kid could have – I have known that for 17 years- craig*

\* \* \*

Gina was very proud of the crèche, and rightfully so. I already understood how unique it was, but to give me a frame of reference, she asked me to accompany her on a trip into town to see a few other orphanages. It would put the features of her facility into some context, and give me an opportunity to compare. Frankly, I could have just trusted her on the subject. How could anything be better than Enfant de Jesus? And besides, I was having such a great time with the kids and I didn't really want to go into Port-Au-Prince and have to dodge another potential kidnapping. But tagging along was the respectful thing to do, and I felt I better start setting a good example for my future kids.

After another hearty and delicious breakfast I joined Gina and Antoine in the truck headed back down the long, rocky dirt road. Gina told me the first stop was going to be the general hospital in Port-Au-Prince and from there we would go to another orphanage. "It should be a short and easy trip."

It was the first time I knew Gina to be wrong.

If you think finding parking in New York City or any other densely-populated American city is challenging, you should try finding a parking space in central Port-Au-Prince. The population density of Haiti is more than nine times that of the United States. The only parking near the hospital meant we would have to double park, which seemed like an OK thing to do, since everyone else was doing it.

We entered into a side door of the general hospital. Gina flashed an official document and we were waved through. Shortly after we gained entrance, Gina shook hands with a doctor and other staff members, and we went down a hallway to the ward for abandoned children. Of all the things I had seen so far in Haiti, the general hospital's wing for abandoned children was the most horrifying. I wish I could shake from my mind the things I saw there that day.

The conditions were filthy. Flies filled the thick, humid air of the hallways. Deranged children, born addicted to drugs, stood screaming in their cribs like lunatics. Deformed kids missing limbs and other body parts cried out for someone to comfort them. A nurse showed me a baby whose mother had tried to abort with a coat hanger. The child looked like a monster. I had always thought I was pretty tough, but the experience was more than I could handle. My system began to shut down and I could no longer speak. At times I couldn't breathe. I wanted to run away as far as I could. But we were just getting started.

As the tour continued my eyes and ears were filled with horrific sights and sounds. Screams of anger and cries of pained children tore into my mind. After that day, I swore I would never take my life for granted again. No experience in my life was more desperate than the walk through that hospital. I was so upset I don't even remember returning to the truck. When I realized where I was I just sat there, slumped into the back seat, numbed by the experience. When we started rolling again I stared ahead into the crowded streets, catatonic. Gina looked back at me. She had seen the look on my face before. She softly told me we were on our way to another orphanage.

We crept along narrow and reeking streets, and at last found another illegal parking spot in front of an old, multistory building. Like my own emotional state, everything in this town seemed to be deteriorating. With all due respect, the orphanage was a dump. I did not need a complete tour of the facility to reach that conclusion. Poorly-clad children were crammed into rooms with very little to occupy them other than biding time. My guess is they passed their days in non-stimulated subsistence, getting just enough food each day to survive until the next day came along.

As we went through the facility we encountered a girl whom Gina had seen two weeks earlier up the street at another orphanage run by a Catholic priest named Monsignor Peterson. Gina said Peterson had promised to sign the little girl over to her so she could be adopted. She was a beautiful little girl with a round face that lit up when I smiled at her. Gina shook her head in disgust, concerned the girl would be stuck in living conditions far below those of Enfant de Jesus, with no chance of adoption.

A nun giving us a tour of the orphanage was doing a poor job of showing us around the place. Gina appeared to be preoccupied, perhaps over the little girl, or maybe because the nun was doing such a bad job. Gina soon declared: "Thank you, sister. We have seen enough."

She turned to me. "Come on, Craig, we have somewhere else to go."

"Where are we headed, Gina?"

"We are going to pay a visit to Monsignor Peterson. I need to have a few words with him about commitment."

# Chapter 8

## Desperate Lines

The orphanage Peterson ran was just up the street, and we probably could have walked there faster than we arrived by car. Gina was wound up and I hurried behind her as she barreled up to the front door of another rickety building. I could tell from the minute we walked in the door the place was a bare-bones operation. It looked similar to the last orphanage, a little smaller and a little more crowded; the visual opposite of Gina's crèche in Larmardelle.

A young girl whom I believed to be a staff member but could just as easily have been one of the older orphans opened the door and let us in. Gina had been there before and conveyed ease in her actions and responses. Monsignor Peterson entered the room to greet us. Slight, built like a jockey, the priest saw Gina's look and his face turned red. We greeted each other and simultaneously noticed a little baby wrapped in a blanket propped up against the wall in a corner of the room. The child was sick and pale but the features of his face were like a tiny angel, except for a rash that covered most of his pale forehead. I was not very experienced at this, but my quick assessment told me the infant didn't have many more days left. Once I looked past his current condition and studied his eyes and his core features, I saw how beautiful he was. His eyes were alert, and it looked to me like they were crying out for help.

"What is he doing here?" Gina asked in a harsh and forceful tone. She was already worked up about the little girl that was stuck at the last orphanage, and the poor health of the little baby in the room aggravated her brewing frustration.

Monsignor Peterson took a few steps back, obviously on the defensive. He knew he had crossed the line with Gina regarding the little girl, and now he had to quickly explain the pitiful condition of this little boy. Peterson seemed a very tired and defeated man, and I could see how the strain of the work within the confines of the demanding environment had taken its toll on him. I wondered how long he had been trying to care for orphans. It looked like it had been too long. Had there been a white flag in the room, he would have picked it up and waved it.

He looked up at Gina, and in a resigned voice said, "Someone in town brought him here. He is not in good shape and it is a struggle to care for him with all of the other challenges we are having around here right now." He looked away and back down at the floor, clearly demoralized.

Gina went over and scooped up the baby off the floor. She held him tight, giving him a big dose of love. She rubbed his head and looked at him as if to say, "Everything is going to be OK now," and then, without warning, handed him to me.

I believe it was the first time I had held a newborn baby. Other than his rash, I thought the little guy was cute, and he sure was tiny. There was something indescribably unique about him. His frail little hand grabbed on to my thumb and gripped it as tight as he could, as if he was hanging on to it for dear life.

Gina and Peterson began speaking in Creole, and although I could not completely understand what they were saying, I could tell what they were talking about. Gina challenged him as to why the baby was there in the first place. Apparently the newborn had been abandoned on a doorstep down the street. Someone had just laid him down and run away. An unknown person found him on the doorstep and ended up taking him to the logical place: An orphanage. Unfortunately, this particular orphanage housed much bigger kids and did not have the staff or resources to care for a baby properly. He was a newborn puppy thrown in with the big dogs and it was obvious that under the circumstances he didn't have much of a chance of surviving.

The room went quiet and the three of us stood there looking at the baby in my arms. I was perfectly content holding the little guy. Then the priest looked straight at me, waved his hand in my face and said in English, "I change my mind. Baby stay here!"

Gina immediately understood what that meant ... but I didn't. Desperate people do desperate things.

Monsignor Peterson was in desperate need of money -- all you had to do was to look around and you could tell that. Assuming I was a wealthy American, Peterson now wanted me to pay him for the baby, and his outburst was his way of beginning the negotiation.

Unfortunately for Peterson, Gina -- who was agitated even before we walked into Peterson's place -- was now furious at him. The little boy was being neglected either by choice or by circumstance and was on the verge of dying. Asking for compensation for the baby was unthinkable. Gina lost her cool and launched a tirade in Creole, which it was easy to get the gist of.

Peterson's face fell and he looked even more defeated than a few minutes earlier. He no longer had the will to put up an argument. Realizing he looked very foolish, he backtracked and bowed his head. "You are right, you can take care of the baby," he muttered, again in English, clearly for my benefit. "I cannot … I mean … things have been very hard here lately." He pursed his lips and fought back tears.

Gina instructed me to take the baby to the car before Peterson changed his mind. She said she would catch up with me as soon as Peterson signed legal authority over the child to her and the crèche. I took the child through the front door knowing if he were to survive, Gina had saved him. Right then it hit me. Gina and Lucien were real-life heroes. Everyday they were saving kids' lives, and this weak little bundle in my arms was the latest, vivid example of their mission in life.

We immediately got some clean water into the boy and started the long drive back to the crèche. He drank a healthy dose of water and then slept for the entire ride.

His complexion was so light I wondered if he were native Haitian. Gina explained to me that his lack of color was from extreme dehydration and if all went well his color would improve over the next few months. We carried him through the front door of the crèche to the surprise of the staff. They huddled around, anxious to see the baby, and they quickly fed him and gave him a bath. They had a perfect brand new pair of pajamas that someone had donated some time earlier and they got him dressed for bed. By that time he had already begun to look like he had a new lease on life. His life had changed that afternoon. He had come to a place that would take good care of him.

Following Gina's lead, the staff started calling the baby Little Craig. As he was the only infant at the crèche, he became the talk of the staff, which instantly fell in love with him. While the children slept, a few of us had a quiet dinner and reflected on a very eventful day. After dinner I quietly went into the nursery to look at Little Craig. He was sound asleep in peace and contentment. It had been another exceptional day for me in Haiti. The range of experiences was mind-boggling, and I had to share some of it with Kathi.

*today was an unbelievable day- I really don't know where to begin- first of all the trip into PAP was full of sights and sounds and smells that people in America don't experience…imagine a scene from a movie where they are showing a street bizarre in India or China with a zillion people packed into very narrow streets- that is what down town port au prince is like- at times our car was traveling less than a mile an hour- barely creeping…. the currency here looks like a barter system with everything for sale goats..chickens…pigs…I saw a lady carrying live chickens in a huge tin wash bucket on her head- this place is a long way from the internet commerce age….but commerce is going on, a pig for a goat kind of commerce- I have never felt in danger although I could see how it would be very easy for something bad to erupt in these streets- so far my experience with the Haitians has been great- they are a very gentle and attractive group of people…remember when we went to Greece a few days after 9-11 and the news blew the potential of danger way out of whack- that is what I think has happened here- I hope I am right about that.*

*We did a lot today- went to the hospital and orphanages (this orphanage is very different than the ones I saw in pap)- I saw things today that I will never forget….deformed kids, disfigured kids, crippled kids, the images I saw will go a long way to expanding my humanity and from this point forward if I ever complain about anything you are instructed to give me a good whack…..*

*Long story…but we brought a two month old (we think) baby back to the orphanage tonight- he was at a catholic orphanage downtown, a complete dump, and was not being taken care of- I think because he is so young and the rest of the kids were much older – 8-14 yrs –he is very frail and very dehydrated… gina talked the priest into letting us take him back to the orphanage- they did the paperwork on the spot – once we got here all of the staff and gina started calling him little craig…gina thinks has as a really good chance of surviving now that he is here- I know you have said all along that you do not want an infant.but this is going to be a magical kid-my gut tells me he is going to be a real fighter… you should see how tight he held onto my thumb when I was holding him*

*I am going to spend tomorrow with amelec and esperancaia*

*– all of the kids here are so much healthier than the ones I saw today- today I saw and experienced things that will make me a better man, and thru it all I kept saying I wish kathi was here, but in a way I know you are-*

*I love you – craig*

Over the next few days Little Craig showed dramatic improvement. One morning I was up early -- the roosters were on a rampage, determined to block my efforts to sleep. Gina had also risen early, and she directed one of the cooks to make us an early breakfast. I told her she had to be very proud with all she is doing for these kids. I was in awe of the contribution she was making to the children of Haiti. I told her that I occasionally read or heard about people like her but I have never met one in person, and it was an honor to be having breakfast with her. We began discussing Little Craig, and how precious he was, and that we both felt he was now going to make it. She stopped, took a deep breath and stared straight into my eyes.

"You know, Craig, there was a reason you were there with me the other day when we found the baby," she began. "There is an explanation for what happened and why it happened. Finding Little Craig was no accident, it was part of the plan." She paused for a moment and after a deep breath declared, "Little Craig is your son."

I just sat there staring at her. She didn't flinch; she just stoically stared back at me. No matter how hard I tried to come up with something, I couldn't find an argument for her revelation. First of all it is pretty hard to argue with an unofficial saint, and maybe deep down in my heart I knew she was right. But I had a practical problem.

"Gina, you need to know something. Before I left, Kathi and I agreed I wasn't going to find any kids for us on this trip unless it was so obvious that it was something that happened naturally. I really came here to see the orphanage and to see if and how we could help you. Esperancia and Amelec represented something special to me and they were obvious and unique cases. I have been communicating with Kathi and she clearly trusts and understands the circumstances surrounding those two. But Gina, in all of our previous discussions you need to know that Kathi adamantly opposed us adopting an infant. She has consistently said that babies are a lot of work and we are just too old to keep up with the demands. It is just something that she does not want to do at this stage of her life, and she has been really clear in communicating that to me."

Gina interrupted me. "Craig, sometimes things just defy the gravity of logic." That was that. She got up to refresh her cup of coffee and I went back to the office and sent another e-mail to Kathi.

After an e-mail volley between us, we ended up giving Little Craig the name Quinn Lucien Juntunen. Some of the staff continued to call him Little Craig but from that day forward he was our son, Quinn. I had been in Haiti less than ten days and I violated the "I-am-not-going-to-fall-in-love-with-any-kids" pledge three times over. It was a good thing the trip was going to last only two more days. Had I stayed much longer I would have wound up in the market for a bus.

*Kathi - today amelec, esperancia and I took a walk holding hands around the complex, then all the children joined us on the field. I was running around and amelec was throwing the ball to me (overhand). He has a good arm and can throw- he is not as good at catching the ball and the entire time esperancia looked on adoringly, she is already daddy's little girl.*

*    esperancia now is my shadow and always reaches her hand out for me to hold…she is going to be a gem, sweet, patient and loving……very stable and peaceful…---amelec on the other hand is very emotional and everyone knows what he is feeling, highly expressive and I think he is pretty smart…he picks up English words very quickly.*

*    And our little quinn is looking healthier every day and he is being cared for in an unbelievable way- we gave him a birthday based on how old the doctor thinks he is and his blood tests came back- he is perfectly healthy- it is a miracle that he came back clean- which means we have the go ahead to adopt him…I know he was not part of the plan…but then again… maybe he was in it all along and we just didn't know about it. I don't know about all of this meant to be stuff…but it is hard to argue with the way in which all of this has happened…maybe it is just that it is time for the five of us to become a family…..*

Prior to my arrival, Gina and Lucien had planned a dinner to entertain the head of the Haitian adoption process. They invited me to join them and said I could bring Esperancia and Amelec along. The dinner was a good two-hour car ride away which seemed like a tough trip for the kids. Before dinner Gina brought each child separately into a sitting room to tell them that I was going to be their father. Esperancia came in first and she sat on my lap while Gina explained to her that I was her dad and that Kathi and I would take care of her forever. Esperancia jumped off my lap and gave me a big hug and would not let go. I had tears in my eyes and so did Gina.

She joyfully skipped into the other room. Lucien brought Amelec in for the news and his reaction was even bigger and more energetic, typical of Amelec. He gave me a bear hug and he was laughing and smiling and holding on to different parts of me while Gina continued to explain what all of this meant. We were all going to have to be patient, she cautioned, because there was a lot of paperwork that needed to be done before we could all go home together.

Dinner was a very joyous occasion and a spectacular meal, highly inconsistent with the abundant poverty of the normal Haitian life. This was also my first shot at functional fatherhood. The head of the Haitian adoption process, Mr. Cadet, was thrilled to be part the experience and he took great joy in seeing me interact with Esperancia and Amelec. The kids made my first situation as a parent very easy. Both were well-behaved, with perfect manners. The orphanage had trained them very well, and an occasion like this allowed their manners to shine. I realized that with these kids I had a running start as a dad, and I had Gina and all of the Aunties to thank for that. The three of us held hands out to the car after dinner. It was an evening I will never forget.

*Kathi – we won the lottery with these kids…. imagine a two and a half hour car ride (in the heat) eating at a fancy dinner table with adults and adult food (which was out of this world) and another two and a half hour car ride home…they were like little adults…very fun little adults…before dinner Gina and lucien told both amelec and esperancia that I am their dad and that there mom will be coming to see them soon- it was one of the most special and memorable moments of my life- they both were so happy and excited- I spent some of the ride home trying to figure out what is different about these kids from other kids I have met at home- they are so well behaved and so mature for their age... I think because they went through something so rough at an early age combined with the discipline that they have at the crèche they are very steady and happy. It is more than obvious that they are not spoiled- how could they be....I know one thing – these are our kids, since you are not here it is hard to explain the connection – I have had such a magical day with the kids...I have learned a lot and my perspective has changed...Haiti has been good in that regard. I can't wait to bring you down here and show you the village and the children....there is a sense of importance within these doors and I am impressed with what is being achieved here*

*I love you kathi and the fact that we are now going to raise these kids together i also love the significance of that proposition, you would have been proud of my parenting skills today ... sleep tight baby ... i will be dreaming of you and our new family and all that lies ahead*

*craig*

It was time for me to return home. I was looking forward to seeing Kathi and reliving the dimensions of this experience with her in person. It was very hard to leave Amelec, Esperancia and Quinn. The Aunties knew I was leaving and allowed Amelec and Esperancia to stay up later than the others so we could have some more time together. We went outside to take a walk around the play yard while the other kids were getting ready for bed. We sat on one of the rocks that forms the perimeter of the grass and watched the sunset. Amelec and Esperancia were sitting on the opposing legs of my lap, chewing on sugar cane and spitting the rind out between my feet. It was a poignant moment, a moment of magic. I felt like a dad and a part of a family with these two. As the sun disappeared and created a brilliant sunset, I was basking in the glow.

My practical side wondered when reality would hit and how hard the reality would be. I was savvy enough to know that the euphoric energy of the beginning would fade and the practical reality would bring a drastic end to the self-absorbed lifestyle I was accustomed to. I could see it was going to be a challenge and I hoped at that moment I would have enough gas in the tank to make it. I was 51 years old, and I realized that by the time Quinn would graduate from high school, I would be one click away from 70.

I got up early the next morning and the Aunties had woken Esperancia, Amelec and Quinn so I could say goodbye. We went into the yard and sat on the rock that we had sat on the night before. One of the Aunties gave me Quinn and the four of us cuddled together, anticipating the times that lay ahead. They knew I was leaving. We could not say much to one another, so we just enjoyed each others' company on the rock for a few minutes. Gina came out and translated my goodbye to them. I tried to communicate I had to go back home to prepare for their arrival, and I would be coming back soon with their new mother. I told them I would miss them and that I would think about them everyday. Esperancia seemed to take it in stride, but Amelec was devastated. He had really become attached to me, and there were no real male figures for him on a daily basis in the crèche. I gave Amelec the best hug I could and I tried to tell him not to worry. I kissed Quinn on the forehead and we looked into each other's eyes. It was a look similar to the one we had given each other on the day I met him. In a few days he had become a different kid. He was a healthy baby and I knew he was going to make it. The Aunties led the three of them to the doorway of the crèche as my last bag was thrown into the cage on the back of the truck. As Antoine drove us away, I looked out the back window and waved good-bye one more time to Gina, Amelec, Esperancia and Quinn, wrapped in the arms of one of the Aunties. In Kathi's last e-mail she said some things are just meant to be. Looking back at them I saw my new family, and realized that in a few months I will finally find out what kind of father I was meant to be.

# Chapter 9

## City Lights

Kathi and I spent the summer anxiously awaiting the news our international adoption process was complete and that we could go down to Haiti to bring our children home. We couldn't wait. I had been to Haiti three times and Kathi twice to visit them and even though they were thousands of miles away they already felt like our kids. Kathi was gushing with excitement. Espie's and Amelec's rooms were being decorated and Quinn's sleeping area was constantly being touched up just to "keep it fresh." We envisioned the joyous moments we would experience as a new family.

Every week we said to each other *this* would be the week the papers would finally be completed. But things kept dragging on, which is par for the course in international adoption. Trying to adopt children from another country, especially a Third World country, is analogous to standing in line at the Department of Motor Vehicles everyday for a year. On August 20, 2006, we finally got the call. Everything was done and the passports and visas had been issued. Kathi and I had become parents to three beautiful children, and although we were old enough to be their grandparents and we had no idea what we were getting ourselves into, we looked at the moment as one to celebrate. We went out to dinner, counting it as one of the last romantic moments we would have for a while. At the time, that was OK with us.

We arrived in Haiti a few days later to pick the children up and bring them home. Kathi and I were now officially on the job. Parents. The reunion with our three kids was joyous, yet awkward at the same time. Although we were an instant family, it didn't mean we instantly became a family. Love is not an emotion triggered by a few government stamps and official seals.

Trust, respect and bonding require time and, even though we were all excited to be together, none of us knew exactly how to behave in a situation like this, especially me. But now that we were together, and the emotion of the greetings and the teary hugs were behind us, we had to try to function as a family.

Our first task was to get the kids on a plane to our home in Scottsdale, Arizona, hopefully without incident. The children had never been on a plane. In fact, they had never even been on an elevator. Almost everything they were about to experience over the next few months would be a first for them -- the first ice cream, first hot shower, first Coca-Cola. Now that we had their small hands in ours we realized no one had told us what to do or what to expect. There was no manual for situations like ours. Kathi and I looked at each other the way astronauts must look at each other right before lift off and our eye contact said: "Here we go. Hang on."

When I owned my company I traveled more than I wanted to, but I typically flew first class to ease some of the pain of air travel. I hated traveling, and my way of dealing with it was to find the best sanctuary I could -- a seat tucked away into a corner of the first row with a book or a newspaper. Over the years I would see young parents pulling their screaming kids on to the plane and down the aisle to a row way in the back, dragging the required paraphernalia behind them, scuffing the sides of the seats and passengers along the way. The expression on the parents' faces created the appearance that they were suffering from severely herniated discs and under my breath, I would always say the same word to myself: "Nightmare."

So, as we shuffled our way onto the tarmac and up the stairs of the plane, a realization whacked me like a two-by-four over the head. All those magical child-rearing moments Kathi and I had dreamed up during our dinner conversations that summer had quickly been blown away by the unforgiving wind of reality. We had become one of "those families" I used to see on my business flights. And of course, we were dragging all the kid paraphernalia behind us to prove it.

One of about a hundred practical problems we had underestimated was that our children did not speak English. Further complicating matters was that we did not speak Haitian Creole. We found out in a matter of minutes that was not of minor consequence. We did have one thing in our favor, our seats were in first class, Row 1, and I could see how other parents traveling with young kids would say we were cheating.

As we waited our turn in the funnel to go up the steps, I tried to explain to Amelec and Esperancia this was going to be fun. I pointed to the airplane and said "avion" which is one of the few Creole words I had memorized. They both looked at me as if they wanted to trust me, but something inside them told them not to. I believed they were 49 percent excited and 51 percent scared, which netted out to an "I am not sure if I really want to get on that avion with you" mentality.

Once we got to the top of the steps and on to the plane, Row 1 looked very comforting, since we didn't have to walk a gauntlet of glares and sympathetic glances to get to our seats. I pointed to the first seats we saw and we all sat down. The completion of this minor task seemed like a victory and Kathi and I breathed a sigh of relief celebrating our achievements -- to this point -- as parents.

Parenting may be measured in the small incremental gains you make with your children, but frankly, we were naïve thinking we had conquered anything by safely securing ourselves in our seats. As rookies, we were over-emotional and desperate to cling to anything that looked like we knew what we were doing. Especially by that point, since Esperancia's mental state had deteriorated to a 5 percent excited and a 95 percent scared-to-death status. The door of the plane hadn't yet closed and she had a death grip on both of her armrests and her head locked into a straightforward position. Her escalating fear began to derail Kathi, who made her first rookie mistake by taking everything personally. Kathi was interpreting our brand new daughter's worsening condition to mean she was failing as a parent.

I tried to ease some of the tension by enthusiastically telling her she did a "great job" of finding a spot for our abundance of stuff in the overhead bins.

The compliment did little to ease her stress level. Esperancia was petrified, Quinn was shrieking and Amelec kept buckling and unbuckling his seatbelt in rapid-fire order to entertain himself, annoying many of our fellow first class passengers. As a result, my wife was rapidly losing self-assurance, and we were still only in the boarding process. Those wonderful visions of parenthood Kathi and I had dreamed up back in the summer were fading away. Our first dose of the real action, and we were learning what everyone else knew -- parenting is a lot harder than it looks.

Once we finally took off, the tide turned. Quinn quieted down, Esperancia took her fingernails out of the armrests and Amelec quit playing with the seatbelt and seemed to be content looking out the window to the sights below. Kathi got up to go to the bathroom and all the color returned to her face. I took a deep breath.

It was right about then that the pilot banked to the right and flew over the coastline of Haiti, heading out over the Caribbean Sea. As I looked down at the coastline, I wondered if any of the kids would ever go back. I wondered if years from now they would remember this dreadful place and, as bad as some of the conditions were in Haiti, I wonder if they would even miss it. For a few seconds -- I am ashamed to admit -- my thoughts drifted and I began to wonder what hole my golf buddies were on right at that moment ... I also wondered if there would be a day the kids considered the extreme detour Kathi and I had taken to be on this plane with them.

\* \* \*

We spent the night in a hotel in Fort Lauderdale and it was on to Phoenix the next day. If you don't count Amelec falling into the swimming pool on our way to dinner, and then my jumping in the pool to pull him out with my slacks and designer shirt on, or our feeding Quinn the wrong type of baby food, giving him terrible diarrhea for 36 hours, or not buying enough diapers for Quinn and his unbelievable diarrhea, or Amelec vomiting up into the deep end of the pool the red Gatorade I had given him just prior to throwing him around in the deep end of the pool, or running out of clean outfits for Quinn who kept ruining the ones he had on because of his diarrhea, or that once the kids had their first elevator ride they wanted to spend the rest of the night riding up and down in it, or our taking the kids to the ocean in the morning before the plane ride home only to have a pound and a half of sand get lodged into Quinn's Afro (which took us a good hour to wash out) or our plane to Phoenix being delayed by more than two hours, or the fact that Kathi and Quinn spent the bulk of the flight home in the bathroom trying to ration a dwindling supply of diapers, the rest of the trip home was without incident.

When we got off the plane in Phoenix, exhaustion slammed us -- even Esperancia, who had just slept for the entire four and a half hour flight. The emotions tied to the trip had overloaded our systems. Quinn's stomach had finally settled down, and going into the last leg of our journey he at last had a peaceful energy about him. He fell asleep as we walked through our home airport. We staggered our way to baggage claim.

By now we had learned to communicate using one-word commands and hand signals. The commands were similar to the ones we would give our dogs, complete with accompanying hand signals. "Go" followed by a flick of the fingers forward. "Stay" or "Stop" followed by a palm out or "Wait" reinforced by waving one of our hands horizontally. This form of communication probably fails the test of sensitivity training, but for the time being, it was effective, and all we had.

It was now 7 p.m. Phoenix time and we had a 40-minute car ride to get us home to the hills of North Scottsdale. Over the course of the last two days, I had imagined how demanding this must be for the children. Most of what they were seeing they were seeing for the first time. Our way of life was new to them. They had never taken an escalator ride, never walked up to a baggage claim carousel. During the last two days they had been intrigued, curious, and inquisitive, but never intimidated by all the new experiences. They laughed and giggled through it all. They appeared to be really happy kids.

Our newly-hired nanny was in the car waiting for us at the curb right outside of baggage claim. She was in our new minivan which the salesman at the car dealership dubbed "A Grand Touring Experience," aware I had sworn I would never own a minivan. The only hitch before we could get underway on the drive home was my struggle to secure Quinn in his car seat. I realized suddenly I probably should have practiced with a doll or something over the summer. Unfortunately it was the first time I actually had tried the contraption, and I wasn't doing a very good job. I get it that a car seat is designed for the safety of the baby, but if you want my opinion, this particular model had way too many straps.

It had been a hard trip for all of us, but I think Quinn got the raw end of the deal. First had been the diarrhea caused by the wrong baby food, then came the beach which resulted in a relentless hair-to-sand bonding that almost made us miss our flight. This was followed by my rooting around in his lap trying to secure Strap A into Insert B while an airport cop was barking at me: "Sir, that car must get moving."

Of all of the things the kids saw and did during that trip for the first time ever, it was the shimmering night skyline of Phoenix on the way home from the airport that made the biggest impression. The village that surrounded the orphanage where they came from had no electricity. The expansive landscape of lights left them staring and holding each other's hands in the back of the Grand Touring Experience. I gazed back at them through the rear view mirror and my heart melted. As they leaned against one another, holding hands, they couldn't take their eyes off the sparkling horizon. Maybe the thousands of twinkling lights represented all of the possibilities, good and bad, that were now in front of them. And us.

# Chapter 10

## Homecoming

The trip from Haiti to Scottsdale had been demanding. Now that we were home, however, the real emotional, mental and even physical demands were just beginning. Kathi and I had jumped into parenthood with both feet, although we had no idea how deep the water was.

The expectations of a joyous homecoming were short-lived for two reasons. First, we were all exhausted, and second, our two very large and ill-behaved Labrador Retrievers, Bubba and Buster, came sprinting down the hallway to greet us, which startled the kids. Our dogs were always excited to see us come home from a trip, and this time our arrival was a bigger deal for them because of the kids. The children, already on sensory overload, hadn't seen dogs up close before and they were scared. Bubba and Buster's enthusiasm and Amelec and Espie's fear collided to form a wave of hysteria in the hallway. All of us bunched up and became trapped as we backed ourselves into a corner. Bubba and Buster were in rare form, energetically smelling and licking anything they could get their face on. Their tails were spinning like whirlybirds as they gave the once-over to the new additions to our family. The kids were petrified, and screaming wildly as if they were being attacked by a pack of hungry wolves. Not exactly the homecoming picture we had envisioned.

I finally managed to maneuver the dogs outside into the courtyard while Kathi and our nanny turned more lights on in the house to "warm things up." With the dogs outside, Amelec and Espie relaxed their vise grip on my legs. Their shrieks of fear subsided to gentle sobbing and I rubbed their heads while telling them everything was OK. Kathi walked back down the hall to meet me with Quinn in her arms. We looked at each other knowing we had made a mistake not containing the dogs during our entrance. We had been home just a few minutes and we had already begun to realize that simple procedures and activities would now need a different degree of consideration. As we walked down the hall to show the kids their room, I began to think about all the other things I hadn't thought of before.

For the time being Amelec and Espie were going to share a room and Quinn was going to sleep in his crib in our room. Once the kids got accustomed to their surroundings, we would move them into their own rooms, but for now we wanted everyone to feel as comfortable and as safe as possible. We did our best to show Amelec and Espie around their room, which had a big bathroom, an equally big walk-in closet and two twin beds. Kathi had dressed the beds up with corresponding boy and girl bedspreads. I showed them around the bathroom. They each had their own sink and I demonstrated how the toilet works, which had a different flush mechanism than they were used to. I turned on the shower to let them feel the hot water -- running hot water was another thing they were not accustomed to. I also showed them a few of their clothes Kathi had neatly hung and organized in the closet. Kathi had done an impressive job of preparing the room, with clothes and toys arranged nicely. The bathroom was painted in a tropical scene, complete with monkeys hanging in palm trees along with pictures of all three kids from our early visits to the orphanage. It was a benign unveiling and the room appointments seemed to go unnoticed as the kids were very tired and frankly, still trembling from the affectionate mugging by our dogs.

The tour of the rest of the house could wait until morning. Even as rookie parents we could see the kids were toast. We dressed them in their pajamas, then helped them brush their teeth and wash their faces. We gave them big hugs to welcome them home and send the message -- without words, since it was hard to verbally communicate with them -- "You will be safe here." We tucked them in and dimmed the lights. They were asleep the moment their heads hit the pillow. They looked content and comfortable and I was relieved they were no longer scared. I kept the door cracked open and the hall light on. I leaned on the open door and stood there to watch them drift off. They had been in our care for less than 48 hours, and I was already starting to discover the trust of a child and how expansively beautiful their innocence was.

Two down, one to go. It was time to tend to Quinn and get him ready for his first night in his new crib. We prepared a bottle and after Kathi changed him I rocked him to sleep in my favorite recliner. He, too, sacked right out. I thought about the strides he had made since the moment I met him. Then, he was a child struggling to stay alive. Now, at home in Scottsdale, he was healthy and happy and as far away as he could be from the place where someone had thrown him away. I wondered how this all happened -- how we all ended up together here in Scottsdale. I also wondered how easily it might not have happened. I could see there are thin lines dividing our lives between one reality and another. At one point Quinn straddled a line between life and death. When I met him the line was so thin I could barely see it. I remembered how he grabbed my thumb, pulling himself back from the edge. I could tell in the moment he gripped me, holding on with all his strength, that he was a fighter. And now, as he fell asleep in his new home, on the lap of his new dad sitting in an old chair, I whispered to him that everything was going to be OK. He was home now.

As the children drifted off into heavy slumber, Kathi and I craved our own deep sleep. Before turning in, however, we knew we would have to change our plans for the morning. Kathi had an itinerary all planned out for the day, which seemed to make sense when she was anticipating the day months ago. But now it seemed like way too much. Our biggest mistake would be to overload the kids with forced activities. After a brief discussion we agreed we should just hang out and play it by ear. It was time to get acquainted.

Kathi hates to improvise. She loves agendas and ultra organized silverware drawers. Despite that, she agreed taking it as it comes for the next few days made the most sense. I told her neither of us had any idea what the next day would look like, the only certainty being that I was probably going to have to go over the toilet demonstration once more, and as a family we were not going to be playing the advanced version of *Scrabble* in our first days together.

The biggest certainty was that the next day would be another adventure for all of us. I couldn't start to count the number of things the kids would be seeing and experiencing for the first time. This was a foreign land to them, and all of the modern appliances and gadgets that are integrated into our lifestyle would be part of a crash course of becoming an American kid. I was impressed how they took everything in stride at the hotel, and I hoped things would go as smoothly over the next few days. It had been a long trip home and the cool pillow felt good as I closed my eyes. Being home felt much different tonight, maybe better than ever before. I reached over to hold Kathi's hand. There were lots of things I could have said, but the emotions of the last few days simply said enough. I squeezed her hand and held on as we both fell asleep.

My bliss was shattered about two hours later: Quinn was crying. One of the things I had told Kathi when we were discussing the practical implications of bringing an infant home is that I would, among other things, actively participate in the nighttime diaper changing responsibilities. With Quinn's sounding the alarm, we both quickly sat up from a sound sleep. I told her, "I got it," the way an outfielder calls off another outfielder when running to catch a fly ball, and I briskly hopped out of bed.

During the entire trip home Kathi had changed all Quinn's diapers, and now it was my turn. Frankly I was hoping for a better hour of the day for my inaugural attempt. For the first 51 years of my life this had been an activity I had successfully dodged -- removing a dirty diaper was something I never saw myself doing. But under the circumstances of bringing Quinn home, I knew I would have to man up and do it sooner or later. Now was as good of time as any to answer the bell. However, I was really hoping that he hadn't pooped.

Kathi had set up a changing station on the island of our closet. It was a perfect spot, plenty of walk-around room and with a step up area for storing supplies. Kathi also had told me that at nighttime, we had to change Quinn in the dark. She said any bright light would alert his nervous system that sleep time is over and he would enter a wide-awake state, making it much harder to get him to go back to sleep. He already seemed wide awake to me -- I really couldn't imagine a kid could cry this hard or loud being half asleep -- but I took her word for it and kept the lights off. It was not easy fumbling around in the dark. I felt like a blind third grader trying to land the space shuttle for the first time. So I cheated. I pulled out a flashlight I had planted just for this moment so I could review my work. I got the old diaper off quite easily, and, thank goodness, he hadn't pooped. Getting the new one on required a bit of patience and some ingenuity. I put the flashlight in my mouth so I could use both hands, but

I wasn't sure what represented the back and the front of the diaper. I took a guess and I figured even if I was wrong things would be OK because the A team would be back on the job in the next shift.

Understandably I was a little insecure about my work, and even though I thought I was done, Quinn was still crying. In fact, he was starting to cry a little louder. At first I thought I might have put the diaper on upside down and it was pinching him in a bad spot, but an inspection with the flashlight told me the diaper looked fine. I couldn't get him to stop crying though. I tried lots of things -- I rocked him, we sat in my old recliner so we could lie flat, I sang to him -- nothing worked. I was exhausted and growing frustrated. I was even a little hungry, and then it finally dawned on me that Quinn also might be hungry.

He devoured his bottle. Poor little guy, that was all it was -- he was hungry. And the moment he was full he fell right back to sleep. It sure would have been a lot more efficient if he had just told me he was hungry. His inability to verbally tell me what he needed was something we were going to have to live with for a while. That statement would hold true for his older siblings as well.

I managed to get back to sleep after I reviewed the diaper-changing procedure in my head a couple of times. Soon we were awakened again, this time by the sound of a slamming door. Again, we both jolted up to a sitting position and looked at each other with "uh oh" eyes and I jumped out of bed to run down the hall to see what had happened. The door to the older kids' bedroom was tightly shut. I opened it and turned on the light. Espie was still in bed, sound asleep. I heard a rustling sound in the closet. It had to be Amelec. I turned on the closet light and, sure enough, found Amelec standing in the corner, facing the wall, peeing onto a pair of shoes. In my sleep-deprived state I struggled to understand what he was doing. Then it occurred to me he was standing in the same corner of the closet where the toilet is in the bathroom. He was in the right spot, but in the wrong room.

I quickly tried to stop him without sounding angry or mad. After all he wasn't peeing on my shoes. We were both caught off guard by what was happening and it was pretty certain to me he was still half asleep. I grabbed him by the hand and took him around to the toilet so he could finish what he had started. He was in a zombie-like trance so I skipped any attempt to explain to him why he should be peeing here and not on the shoes in the closet. Once he was done, and he really had to go, I led him back to bed. I picked up the shoes in the closet, threw them in the shower and made a halfhearted attempt to clean things up.

I closed the door to the bedroom and sat down on one of the steps in the hallway. Too tired to cry, I began to laugh as I muttered to myself, "Welcome to parenting, Craiger." I might just as easily have said farewell to sleep. Right then Quinn woke up again, crying. I took the few steps back into our bedroom, told the A team to go back to sleep, and said I would take care of him. Then I headed straight to the closet to find the flashlight.

# Chapter 11

## First Days

Kathi's itinerary for our first day at home was shelved, reduced to fuel for a future winter fire. That eliminated the pressure to create a picture-perfect first day at home. As we had discussed last night, we were just going to hang out around the house and get acquainted. I felt more confident with our new strategy, as I figured anybody could be successful doing that.

Despite the fact I had had very little sleep the previous few days, and had been up with Quinn most of the last night, I still woke before dawn. First game jitters.

The first order of business was to sequester the dogs to the guesthouse. We did not want a rerun of "Terror in the Hallway" that premiered last night. I gave them their morning treats in the usual spot outside of our bedroom, and we began the walk over to their new detention quarters. I put them inside the three-room guesthouse and told them everything was just going to be fine. I halfheartedly tried to convince them this new arrangement was just for a few days. Over the years our dogs could not have been more loyal companions. They would have limped up Mount Everest by my side, if that was where I was going. Now it seemed inevitable I would have to betray their loyalty, and that hurt. I rubbed both their heads, knowing our relationship was forever going to change. I could barely look them in the eyes.

For 11 years these loyal companions had been the focus of our attention and they defined the term "Best Friends." Kathi and I were "over the top" dog people and Bubba and Buster were the center of our universe. We never got them matching sweaters or anything goofy like that, but as much as dogs could be, they were one of our key priorities. From that day forward it would no longer be true. In my wildest dreams I never imagined I would be shutting them out, but as I closed the door, with them now confined to the guesthouse, that is exactly what I was doing. I took a slow, melancholy walk back to the main house … to a new life, the one in which our top priorities were still sound asleep.

I went over to check on Quinn and he was parked in dreamland. Even sound asleep, with his two middle fingers shoved into his mouth and a stream of drool sliding down his cheek, he still looked like a little angel to me. The lights were down and there was a peaceful quite to the house, a state that in the future I would come to appreciate more and more, and experience less and less.

As I fired up the coffee maker, I was more than a little uneasy about how this was going to work out. Not just today, but everyday from there on. It was the beginning of something very different. Imagine having been in a career, say, as an accountant, for most of your life. Then one day you woke up and, presto, you had become a brain surgeon. And as they rolled the patient into your operating room, there was no one around to tell you how to make that first incision. Maybe being a dad isn't brain surgery. But then again, maybe being a *great* dad is. At that point I was not sure if I would ever be great at fatherhood. I was thinking only about surviving, and my apprehension stemmed from the fact I had no idea of what functionally made up a good dad. Somehow I would have to quickly figure that out. I at least wanted to live up to my end of the bargain.

I supposed the first step was getting acquainted, and that was going to take some time, especially with the language barrier. I was anxious to get to know these kids. All I had to go on now were first impressions, and first impressions are nearly always misleading. All of us had been on our best behavior during the four short trips we made to the orphanage and our trip home from Haiti. But now that we were home, we would all naturally gravitate to the core of who we really were.

Included in my first impressions of the kids was that they were attractive and fun to be around. Just as he does now, Amelec had a very athletic build; in fact he was very stocky with defined muscles beyond his early age. He was built like a mini-linebacker, and if I were a Pee Wee football scout I would have described him as thick, which was rare among Haitians, who mostly are lean and willowy. Back then, as now, he had an extremely happy disposition, a great smile and an even better laugh, good assets for him because he smiled and laughed a lot. I could see he was very social and seemed very comfortable in every setting we put him into. During dinner at the hotel in Fort Lauderdale, Amelec became fascinated with a man playing a piano. I took him up to the piano so he could get a closer look, and if he had been asked, he would have sat down and started singing a duet. I saw Amelec as charming, outgoing, and charismatic, at levels advanced for his age and for a newcomer in a foreign land.

At the other end of the spectrum, Espie appeared to be introverted and far less outgoing. During our trips to the orphanage I had observed her playing by herself or simply tidying up around her bed. Whereas Amelec was more than willing to reach out and engage in a social circumstance, Espie stood back, observed, and was much more cautious. She was dainty in stature, but certainly not frail. In fact she also had the beginnings of a sharply-defined muscle structure, and it looked like she was going to be very tall and lean. She was and is a beautiful girl with high cheekbones and big moon-shaped eyes that are hauntingly expressive. The Aunties had styled her hair in cornrows right before she left the orphanage, a hairstyle that greatly played up the elegance of her facial features. When Kathi put her in a dress for dinner the first night at the Fort Lauderdale hotel she looked like a little movie star. Most of all she appeared to be very bright and perceptive. Nothing got past her, and I believe she understood what a big break she had received getting out of Haiti.

We had been told Amelec's birthday was January 16, meaning he was 5 when we adopted him, and Espie's was September 21, meaning she was 4. It was hard to know for certain because, most likely, someone in the crèche had made a guess as to their birthdays. Similarly, Kathi and I had made up a birthday for Quinn. We believed as they grew up and got past their teens their exact birthdays would become incidental to them. We knew Amelec and Espie were close in age, and during the trip home Kathi and I would go back and forth as to which of them appeared -- or more importantly, acted -- older. The paperwork said they were about nine months apart, and we decided we could live with the approximate truth of that.

While Amelec was able to find the joy in nearly everything, Espie was much more discriminating. Both of them laughed at the same things; Amelec just laughed louder and longer. Observing their different and distinct personalities, I envisioned they were going to be very competitive with each other. Although they were not biologically related they began acting like brother and sister from the moment we told them we were going to adopt them. They had both been at the orphanage for more than two years so they already knew each other very well. Given what they had already been through together, they actually might have been closer than biological brothers and sisters. Crisis has a way of bringing people together. It is hard to imagine a bigger crisis than being separated from your parents at an early age and thrown into an orphanage in one of the most messed-up countries in the world. In my mind it was a safe bet the bond between Amelec and Espie would grow stronger as the years went on.

Even though Quinn didn't do much more than poop and sleep and wiggle around on the floor, I didn't need a degree in child psychology to predict his future personality. Quinn was extremely adamant when he wanted something and he wouldn't stop being extremely adamant until he got what he wanted. It was just my luck to have a demanding baby who was stubborn as a mule sleeping in the same room with me, but that's what we had. On the other hand, maybe that explained why he was still alive. Quinn's strong will was already evident and his undeniable and mighty determination was something I was coming to admire, at least theoretically. More practically I loathed it, especially during the middle of the night.

Kathi had woken up while I was returning in dejection from escorting the dogs to their new living quarters, and she joined me for a cup of coffee while the kids continued to sleep. She asked if I was ready for all of this. I had conflicting body language, smiling and shaking my head at the same time. I stammered, "If I am not ready now… at … at … 51 years… I … well … I suppose I will never be ready. And ….besides…. as of now, being ready is no longer relevant. We have only been home a night… but Kath….. once these kids wake up we are way past preparation."

Three cups and plenty of deep breaths later, and there was still not a peep from any of them. It was way past the time they usually woke up at the orphanage. They could not speak English, but they were certainly telling us something. We had three very tired kids in our house. It was a good thing we canned the agenda, otherwise we would already be way behind and Kathi would be beside herself.

All three woke up later that morning and we went about things as slowly and as easily as possible. We took

our time getting them something to eat and drink --
doughnuts, juice, and cut-up fruit -- and leisurely showed
them around the kitchen. They really loved the fruit and
politely nibbled at their doughnuts, which proved my
first prediction as a dad to be wrong -- I had expected
they would devour them. There was more nodding and
smiling than there was conversation, for obvious reasons,
and after breakfast we all just cuddled and laid around in
Amelec's and Espie's room, looking at some of their toys
and books. Quinn gently fell back asleep and I adoringly
put him back into his crib.

The first couple of days were simple -- not easy -- but
simple. We did not do a heck of a lot, but we sure used up
a lot of energy. We had made a strategic decision to give
our nanny the first few days off, so that it would be just
us with the kids. We thought that would avoid sending
any confusing messages to the kids early on. We
lollygagged around the house, slowly introducing them
to a plethora of things they had never seen before -- our
swimming pool, hot tub, garage, the garage door openers,
the dimmers on the light switches (which Amelec thought
were really cool), and other modern-day wonders.

In the past 48 hours it was like they had been beamed
up from a very primitive environment to a very advanced
one. To put their transition from one extreme to another
into some context, they were greatly amused by the "hot"
and "cold" faucets in the bathroom with corresponding
hot and cold running water.

The biggest hit was the TV, at least in short bursts.
Since they couldn't understand what was being said, they
quickly lost interest in the things they were watching and
drifted away to go do something else. But they would

quickly return to the images on the television and act out as much of the action as they could, until they were again overloaded with dialogue, which propelled them in yet a new direction as the cycle repeated itself. The discovery of all of this stuff was a colossal adventure for them, too big to adequately describe. We could see what they were going through, and in response we tried to keep other things -- like meals -- unadventurous and easy.

That first night Kathi prepared a dinner of rice and beans, wisely choosing a cuisine the kids would find familiar. She neatly laid the ingredients onto the kitchen counter in assembly-line fashion, preparing as if she were going to make a gourmet meal. She wore her apron labeled "Cook of the House," which she ordinarily wore only when preparing holiday meals. The significance of the apron was obvious. Now that she was cooking for a family, she was taking the activity much more seriously than when she was just making dinner for the two of us. This was to be the first dinner she would prepare for the kids, and it was clear -- monogrammed apron and all -- it was a big deal to her. Even though the entrée was as basic as rice and beans with some green vegetables on the side, she was still trying to create a masterpiece.

Despite her best efforts and the ceremonial wearing of the apron, the meal was a disaster, at least from the perspective of Amelec and Espie. Of the many variations of rice and beans, she apparently had chosen the wrong one and they both hated it. They picked at their plates and made unpleasant faces. I took turns feeding Quinn and myself. Between bites I could see the disappointment in Kathi's face and in support of her I gently encouraged Espie to go ahead and eat her meal. She responded, without hesitation, by defiantly pushing the plate away from her place setting, and violently shaking her head no.

We had been told by a few of the adoption counselors that at some point the kids would try to test us to determine boundaries in the relationship. That point had arrived with Espie. I tried to correct her disrespectful behavior and said, "We don't do that, Espie. Those are not good manners." I took strides to talk in a calm, non-threatening tone. It was simply a matter of trying to get her to understand the fundamentals of this particular wrong choice. I nudged the plate of food back onto the place-setting in front of her. "Go ahead Espie, please enjoy your meal," I said quietly.

She put another bite of rice and beans in her mouth, looked at me, made a face and forcefully spit the food back onto the plate. At that point my instincts took over. I got up, grabbed her out of her chair, and carried all 37 pounds of her to her bedroom. She gasped, and her skinny legs were running in mid air as she tried to propel herself back to the table. Once we got to her room I dumped her on her bed and told her to stay there. I reinforced the message by using one of my dog signal commands. She was visibly shaken by my reaction and she began shrieking. I slammed the door behind me and marched back to the dinner table.

Amelec, observing how the energy at our first dinner had turned severely negative, was now gutting it out and eating Kathi's version of rice and beans as deliberately as he could. I was upset, tired, and wondering whether I had done the right thing. So I chose to take it out on someone else.

In an agitated voice, I asked Kathi, "How in the world

do you screw up rice and beans?" I followed up by giving her a confused look, as if this whole mess had somehow been her fault. She just shrugged her shoulders and we did the best we could to try to get back to normal. I took a deep breath and put more steak sauce on the remaining portion of rice and beans. Kathi and I restarted the hum of a conversation, but any pleasantries that were offered up were drowned out by Espie's wailing from down the hall.

I am not sure where Kathi came up with some of this parenting stuff, but she sure seemed to know a lot more than me on the subject, and I usually took her coaching at face value. During the summer one of the points she had coached me on was a technique used by many parents called a "timeout." According to Kathi, a timeout is designed to "communicate to the child that they are behaving inappropriately by removing them from their current setting, which gives them a place to safely adjust their frame of mind" or something like that. She went on to say that "An ideal timeout should only last a few minutes and when the timeout is complete, there is to be a discussion about a 'better' type of behavior."

To me, a timeout simply sounded like a touchy-feely version of a punishment I received whenever I screwed up in elementary school: "Go stand in the corner."

I was certainly disappointed in Espie's behavior, even if she did find Kathi's rice and beans recipe uneatable. She had been blatantly disrespectful by spitting it out the way she had. She needed to learn right off the bat disrespectful behavior would not be tolerated in the household. I had called my first timeout on my daughter. It was simply by instinct. And as far as managing the timeout was concerned, I would have had Espie stay in her room until the rest of us were done with dinner, but Kathi kept looking at me anxiously, as if I was holding Espie's head underwater. Since it was our first night and Kathi had read more books on timeouts than I had, I caved in to the worry in her face and went down to retrieve Espie so she could try to finish dinner with us.

I had probably given Espie what amounted to a double time out, which was too long for Kathi and too short for me. Our first family dinner at home had rapidly deteriorated. Amelec looked miserable as he painfully tried to finish his meal. Quinn was shrieking in his high chair, most likely as a demand to get out of his high chair. Kathi and I had just had our first philosophical disagreement about disciplining the kids and she was also irked at me for my unfair rice and beans comment. On top of everything, I now had to go down the hall and have my first father-daughter "talk," complicated by the fact my daughter could not understand what I was going to talk to her about.

Espie had gotten off the bed where I had left her and was now sitting on the floor, whimpering. She looked scared. I decided there were not any appropriate dog-hand signals available for this kind of discussion, so I just sat down with her on the floor and started things off with a hug. That got her sobbing again. I think she understood what she did was wrong. In the gentlest voice I could muster, I tried to explain to her we have a thing called respect and it is important we all respect each other as a family. It is also important that we respect all of the things around us. I told her her mama had worked hard to prepare her a meal and that we were very lucky to have a good hot meal like this to eat. I told her she had to go to her room because what she did was wrong. But even though her actions were wrong, mom and dad still loved her, and we always will. I told her that love is something that is always part of the good times and the bad times.

I knew she couldn't understand the specific words, but I also think that somehow she captured the gist of our "talk." And for good measure, I acted out what she had done, pretending to push my plate away while I was shaking my head, then pretending to spit my dinner out on the table, while making a disgusting face.

After my impersonation, I held both of her shoulders to stabilize her, looked her squarely in the eye, and simply said "NO" which is one word I knew she understood.

I gave her another hug, and while I was hugging her I repeated that even in the bad times I would love her and take care of her and I would always try my best to be a good dad. Then I asked, "You want to join the rest of the family to finish dinner?"

She shyly nodded her head, and stared at me with those saucer-sized eyes. I think it was her way of saying she was sorry. We held hands as we walked back to the dining room. I had just completed my first heart-to-heart talk with one of my kids. I thought it went pretty well, under the circumstances. Maybe it is easier to talk to your daughter when you don't have to worry about her understanding you.

# Chapter 12

## Out and About

After Espie and I sat down, the positive vibe returned to the dinner table, and Kathi even reached out to grab my hand. Espie politely ate the rest of her dinner, which seemed more than acceptable to her this time around. I even helped myself to seconds. Peace had been restored.

Now that our roller coaster of dinner-time emotions had come to a gentle stop, it was time for us to get off this particular ride. I announced, "Let's go take a family walk around the block." I thought we would benefit from a little fresh air, and it looked like the sky was preparing to serve up one of those famous desert sunsets. Kathi and I frequently took Bubba and Buster on after-dinner walks, and I really enjoyed touring the neighborhood with them. But tonight Bubba and Buster were left off the invitation list. We plopped Quinn into his new stroller, which was much easier to strap him into than his car seat. We held hands as we leisurely made our way around the block. Kathi and I rambled on about the spectacular sunset while Espie and Amelec picked up rocks and threw them into the desert. After living through the tension at dinner I said to myself, "This is more like it." Of course the kids weren't saying much of anything as we wandered along. I wondered what they were thinking. I wondered whether they missed watching the sunset with their buddies back at the orphanage.

After a few days hanging around the house we decided to try our luck at a family outing. After all, how much lollygagging around the house can you do before you need some activity? There were plenty of choices in the Phoenix area, which offers a wide range of family-friendly activities. We narrowed our choices down to ice skating, going to the zoo, and -- my choice -- going to a baseball game. Kathi rolled her eyes after that last suggestion, and even I could see the pitfalls in the idea of going to a ballgame, so, in the end, we wound up picking the zoo. The selling points were that looking at animals didn't require a lot of verbal communication, and the activity would involve a decent amount of time.

The children were still drowning in a flood of new things and experiences. In this overwhelmed state they became ultra-dependent on us, and as a result, we had to be with them every waking minute. From the instant they got up to the minute they went to sleep we were at their sides, and we didn't have a moment to ourselves. They were excited, confused and tentative. You couldn't blame them. I didn't know how well any of this had been explained to them before they left the orphanage. After all they were just little kids, and a few days earlier their lives had been confined to the shelter of the crèche. Literally overnight they had become part of a new family, with all the unique and complicated surroundings that accompanied it.

If I had been in their circumstance, I would have been in a much bigger panic than they were. Their reaction to the newness was not panic, but to revel in it by constantly showing us what they were doing and how they were doing it. They had an urgent need for us to approve of what they were doing. If they learned a new word or phrase, we would hear it about 100 times before they would stop saying it. They imitated what they saw on TV over and over again. Kathi and I were the attentive audience, and they were the stars of a grand show as they moved on from one silly performance to the next. Just tagging along and watching was exhausting. All the while we patiently validated their actions and accomplishments by repeating the phrase "Good job," which we essentially wore out before lunch on the first day.

The three of them needed constant, undivided attention, and there were only two of us. Kathi and I were forced into zone coverage, not having enough team members to play man-to-man -- at least until our nanny was back on the job. The numbers evened up temporarily when Quinn was sleeping, but if his early behavior indicated anything, Quinn was going to be a very poor sleeper.

When he was awake, which seemed like most of the time, we struggled to keep up with him and we often had to fish him out of all kinds of places, like the fireplace he crawled up and into the morning we went to the zoo. When I finally got him out of there he looked like a tiny coal miner, with soot all over him and his Superman jumper. The trip to the zoo might possibly give Kathi and me a chance to catch our breath for a few minutes, and provide the kids a chance to get outside for an extended period of time and burn off some of their energy.

During breakfast I showed the kids pictures and gave them names of animals they would see that day. We practiced saying lion, zebra and giraffe. Before I could say the word, Amelec pointed at a picture of a rhinoceros and yelled out in clear English, "Dinosaur!" I don't know where he got that, but he had said it with such enthusiasm and in such perfect English, that for now, Kathi and I decided we would all refer to any rhinoceros as a dinosaur.

At breakfast, it occurred to me Espie had been a little angel at all our meals since that first dinner. After we finished the meal, I kept the kids corralled by the TV while Kathi got us ready to leave the house. It would be the first time the kids had left the house other than our walks around the block and playing within the confines of our gates. They would be seeing the surroundings of the community for the first time. When we arrived three days earlier it was night and all they could really see were twinkling lights and long shadows. Now they would see images far different from the landscape and city streets of Haiti. They wouldn't see people walking down the streets with things stacked on their heads. They weren't going to see dilapidated houses, or half-built buildings that had been abandoned, or acres of filthy, reeking garbage strewn about.

Today they would see finished buildings, with steel and glass and modern architecture. They would see new cars, and businesses and shops where people were buying things. They would see an orderly flow of traffic, a school bus and plenty of other partial perspectives on their future. It would all be unfamiliar, but one thing was certain; by the time we reached the zoo they would know they weren't in Kansas anymore.

Also after breakfast our nanny showed up for work, and Kathi and I breathed a sigh of relief. We were back to man-to-man coverage, which was great news for me. As we loaded up, I could not believe all the bags of stuff we were taking to the zoo. It appeared we were going away for a three-day weekend. I shook my head in wonder at the dramatic change parenting was bringing into our lives. For a second I thought the excess baggage might be attributed to Kathi simply going overboard. More likely, it was another example of how badly I had miscalculated what it took to be a parent. Had we become low-land sherpas? As I closed the hatch of the minivan our nanny told me I looked tired. Well, I *was* tired, but she didn't have to rub it in.

After the Grand Touring Experience was loaded down like a government mule, we strapped in the kids and climbed aboard. I swung out into traffic and began performing the role of tour guide, pointing out everything I could to the kids on the 30-minute ride to the zoo. My part kept me very busy, as there were many things to point out. However, being isolated in the pilot seat of the car brought a relaxing break from the bustle of tending to the minute-to-minute needs of the children. After four days I was starting to feel a little worn down.

In those four days, just taking a bathroom break was a luxury. I hoped things would get easier with our nanny back on the job. They better, or I would have to start looking for a new brand of vitamins.

Only four days into the role of a parent and I was already whining. In our retirement life I had only one person to look after -- me. And frankly, Kathi did more looking after me than I did. With the adoption of the kids, we had moved from Easy Street to Commotion Street overnight. And at that new address I felt like a bug on a hot griddle running back and forth. As I considered the strains of the role I had volunteered for, I wondered, "How do people do this?"

On the other hand, compared with most other parents I was running downhill with the wind at my back. How in the world does a single mom with multiple kids and a full-time job, or maybe two jobs, pull it off? I didn't have the stress or time conflict of a job, I had no financial worries, we had the help of a nanny, and we had only three kids. Only three! I was a parenting wimp.

I began to have concerns about my internal constitution, and I was rapidly acquiring a newfound respect for people who excel as parents. As we arrived and pulled into the zoo, I was a little disappointed we didn't have farther to drive. I had become pretty comfortable perched in the driver seat. I was now partially rested, but fully concerned. Was I really cut out for this? Had I made a mistake?

The zoo was a good distraction from my growing insecurities. Everyone had fun -- even me. We meandered around looking at birds, snakes and monkeys. I discovered there is a common language used while looking at animals – it's called pointing. As each of us saw a creature move out from under a rock we pointed and shared in the experience of a sighting. This was the first common ground we stood on. The hierarchy of our newly-created family had temporarily collapsed, trumped by the joys of pointing at a monkey coming out from behind a hedge.

Our nanny took a break from the action and kept an eye on Quinn while he took a short nap under a big shade tree. Kathi and I took the big kids on paddleboats on a pond in the center of the zoo. As we gently propelled ourselves around the pond, both Amelec and Espie seemed to settle down and relax. It was as if they had taken a huge, deep breath and downshifted. For the first time since we had come home there was calm about them. They had stopped calling out Mama or Papa every other second. It seemed this was the moment for them when things started to sink in. This was for real -- we were a real family. Kathi was their mom and I was their dad.

Maybe their overwhelming and constant need for attention and approval the first few days had been their way of saying they were scared, and didn't want to be abandoned a second time.

I watched them peacefully look around at the things in the lagoon, and as we paddled back to the dock, I yearned for the day they no longer feared they would have to go back to Haiti. I knew it would be a comforting day for them to know for certain this new place, this good place, complete with everything new they were discovering, was the place they could confidently call home.

After the boat ride we reunited with Quinn and our nanny under the shade tree. We bought the kids cotton candy (another first), which Espie quickly devoured and Amelec nibbled on. I don't think Quinn really consumed any of the small portions we gave him; but he did his best to make a sticky mess all over his face and his clothes. We resumed our walk along the pathways of the zoo and watched the various animals' sun themselves and lay around. We were perfecting the technique of the "family point." Soon we came around a corner and saw the rhinoceros pen. One of them stood right in the middle of the pen, as obvious as a big spot of black ink on an empty sheet of white paper. In unison we pointed and shouted, "DINOSAUR!"

We howled in delight, and at that moment we looked -- and more importantly felt -- like a family. In a mysterious way we had shed some of our initial awkwardness, left over there on the other side of the paddleboat pond. Up to that minute our interactions had been a little forced. But this instant was different -- this was casual and we had all let our guard down. Right then it seemed as if we always had been a family and this was just a routine day at the zoo. The day turned out so easy and utterly enjoyable because we had taken an important step on the path toward becoming a family. We shared more than sights and sounds, we shared moments, like families are supposed to. We also had fun communicating with each other using simple phrases and words, beyond just "dinosaur." But the sun was high in the sky and beating down on us, and we were all getting tired. I looked at my watch and knew it was time for this family to head home.

* * *

We felt we had had such success on our first outing, we would double up with another activity the following day. Months before the adoptions were complete, back in the summer when Kathi was busy creating daily itineraries, I did what any other dad would do awaiting the arrival of his children from a Third World country. I went out and bought golf clubs, junior sets for Amelec and Espie.

I started playing golf late in life, something I viewed as a disadvantage. I wanted to get my kids started early, mostly because I believed lessons learned on the golf course were great life lessons. Lessons of honesty, perseverance and managing frustration were just a few of the positive virtues delivered by what I believed to be the world's greatest game. I have always said that golf and character go hand in hand. I can't say for sure that the game of golf builds character, but I know it certainly reveals it.

Maybe the simple job description for being a dad -- in addition to being a provider -- is to be a great role model and a good teacher. Every good teacher benefits from a compelling venue to powerfully reinforce each learning point. For me, golf would be the venue, I would be the teacher, and my kids would be the students. I loved the game of golf so much, I had fantasized about playing it with our kids. I had had many meaningful moments on the golf course with my father, and I wanted to carry on that tradition with my kids. The day had come for that experience to begin.

After breakfast I took Amelec and Espie out to the garage to show them their new clubs. They took to the clubs and golf bags the way they have received everything else, curiously interested but not overly excited or enthused. I could see it would be tricky to explain to two young children the idea of golf and how to use the clubs properly. But I would learn it was basically impossible when they don't speak English. For purposes of damage control, I held off from introducing the golf ball into the mix. I was proud of my discipline, until I looked up and saw Amelec flailing away like a runaway windmill with his new 9-iron in the middle of the garage. A second before he could take dead aim on the sideview mirror of one of the cars, I guided him from the garage and into the wide-open space of the courtyard. I think Amelec and Espie would have had more interest in the golf clubs if I had showed them how to squish bugs with them. Instead I demonstrated the more conventional use, showing them a structured golf swing a few times in courtyard before loading the clubs into the trunk of the car. I don't think either one was paying much attention to my demonstration of the swing, as they seemed to be more interested in examining the many zippered compartments on each of their golf bags.

A little put off that they were not captivated by my pre-lesson, I hollered for Kathi. She bounced out of the house in a coordinated golf outfit, ready for our second outing. I smiled; one of my dreams was about to come true -- I was going to give our kids a golf lesson.

Being the middle of summer, we knew our country club would be a ghost town, creating the ideal setting for a first golf lesson for two kids from Haiti from a rookie parent who had never given a golf lesson before. If this had been the high season and other members had actually been around, Kathi would have been concerned we were disrupting the sophisticated atmosphere at the club. Almost all the members of this particular club were high-brow folks and viewed the facility as their second home or get-away place. Fortunately, that day, the place was deserted. Who in their right mind would play golf in Scottsdale in August?

In the shimmering desert heat a lonely attendant loaded our clubs onto golf carts, probably the only thing he would do that day. The golf carts fascinated Amelec and Espie, and as we drove down to the driving range they paid close attention to every detail of the buggies. It appeared the golf carts were the coolest things they had ever seen, surpassing even their initial reaction to TV. They chuckled and carried on as we wound down the cart path. Between fits of laughter they started calling the golf carts "Petite Machines," which seemed to make things all the more comical.

They seemed a little disappointed when the ride in the Petite Machines ended and the time came to begin the golf lesson. What I learned from the "lesson" is that the chasm between fantasy and reality can seem as wide as the universe itself. The pace and tempo of golf is supposed to be slow and graceful; a physical art form. I quickly discovered that I had no clue how to properly teach a kid a golf swing, and with every coaching point I gave I was brutally reminded that neither Amelec nor Espie could understand what I was saying.

I did my best to patiently show them what to do so they could imitate my actions. But the result was utter chaos, and for Kathi's sake it was a good thing that none of the other members were around, because the kids were well on their way to destroying the driving range. They saw the clubs in their hands as weapons, not instruments of artistry, and they aggressively started whacking away at the earth, as if punishing it for all its evil deeds. I was doing the best I could to contain their primal 8-iron assault and get them to try to hit the ball. Instead of coming across as a guru of the refined art of golf, I looked more like a red-faced drill sergeant, sweating like a pig and frantically shouting out a series of coaching points while the kids forcefully excavated turf and dirt from the pristine driving range. The more I coached, the worse they got, and the idea of having either of them actually make contact with a ball was now a certifiable long shot. On the rare occasion when one of them did make incidental contact with a ball, it would dribble forward a few pitiful feet.

To deflect some of the blame from me, the golf lesson may have been doomed from the start. First of all, I discovered that Amelec is left-handed, or at least has a strong urge to use a left-handed swing. Of course I had bought him right-handed clubs. So everything I showed him was backwards. The poor kid had a lot going against him: A nincompoop for an instructor, a severe language barrier, and having to mimic the golf swing as if looking into a mirror. I also found that Espie is about as coordinated as a newborn deer. Her gawky and non-rhythmic flailing about with a golf club may have been one of the most athletically ungraceful things I have ever seen. While it became clear to me the lesson was a disaster, the good news was that if I needed to find a couple of kids to rototill a garden with golf clubs, I would not have far to look.

I don't know who gave up on the lesson first. After

much swing-and-miss pandemonium, the children looked over to mom, who intelligently had been sitting in the shade on one of the Petite Machines the entire lesson with an "I told you so" look on her face. In the kid's eyes the Petite Machines looked a lot more appealing than continuing the golf lesson with me. Eventually they threw their clubs to the ground and ran over to Kathi as if they were escaping a raging fire. The lesson was over.

I dejectedly tried to clean off the clubs as well as I could so I could return them for a refund, or at least exchange Amelec's set for a left-handed version. The kids were sitting in the driver's seats, pretending to be driving the carts as they sat parked in the shade. Having successfully accomplished the golf lesson mutiny, they looked like they were having fun again. I walked over to join them with my tail between my legs, knowing I had failed as a golf instructor, and even worse, I was probably going to eat the cost of two sets of junior golf clubs.

Since the club was going to be over seeding soon and every other member was in a different time zone, I had a great idea. I put Espie on Kathi's lap in one cart and Amelec and I jumped in the other. I had resigned as a golf instructor, but that wouldn't stop me from teaching them to drive a golf cart. So off we went, right down the grassy hill and into the middle of the driving range. Edging ahead of me, Kathi looked back and said, "See ya!" and floored it. Amelec and I were still cautiously moving down the hill and he looked at me as if I was some sort of sissy. I took his cue, and jumped on the accelerator with everything I had. This was supposed to be a sensible, comfortable ride, but it had quickly turned into full-blown Petite Machine race on the driving range.

The spontaneous game became great fun as our racing around the empty range took on a sort of random precision. Both carts were in sync, and we launched into figure-8s that felt almost choreographed. We let the kids take over steering, and the choreography became a little more elaborate. They had a blast making wild and crazy turns. A few times we just missed crashing into each other. Of course the faster and the more out of control we were, the more the kids loved it. As we would circle and pass each other we made faces and gestured at each other. It was our version of the Crash Cup Derby, although I am proud to say we did no damage to the carts. We did, however, take the golf carts to places they had never been before at that club. The kids were howling and screaming at the top of their lungs … and so were Kathi and I. This was better than a ride at an amusement park, and since there was no one waiting in line we did not have to stop.

The doomed golf lesson had lasted minutes, but the after party on the Petite Machines went on and on. It was a joyous moment, like many in the future I would never forget. Based on the events of the day, I knew it would be a while before I realized my dream of actually playing a round of golf with my kids. In time that day would come. For now, I have learned there are many ways to have fun with your kids. That day I was offered another part of the dad job description, having enough sense to go with the moment.

# Chapter 13

## No Lingering

As we were driving home from the club I felt a little bad that Quinn was not included. Practically he was going to have to be the third wheel, at least for a while, something that would of course change over time. I was amazed by the unique bond he and I shared. Many of our friends had tried to put our connection into a deeper, mysterious context, but I was content to accept it at face value, and did not see any reason to try to explain it.

However, I was also coming to the realization I may have overcommitted with my pledge: "Don't worry honey, I will be there to take care of Quinn at night." When I said that, I didn't realize how little sleep he needed, and I took for granted how much sleep I needed. In the early days I was up with him at least three times a night, with the only real benefit being I was becoming an expert at the diaper-and-feeding turn-around. In fact I had become so proficient at the task I had stopped using the flashlight.

I made a game out of feeding and changing him in the middle of the night. I started informally measuring how fast I could complete the entire procedure and get him back to his crib. I raced the clock with the same concentrated sense of urgency you see in a pit stop in car racing. These middle-of-the-night pit stops involved two tasks: Fill the tank (Quinn downs a bottle); and switch out tires (Craig changes a diaper). Kathi was impressed by my speed, knowing that the faster I completed Quinn's pit stops, the faster we all got back to sleep. Or at least in theory.

Kathi was still adamant the nighttime pit stops had to happen in the dark, so as not to alert Quinn's nervous system it was time to wake up and start putting toys into his mouth. I had yet to see any documentation on this particular methodology, but since he nearly always fell right back asleep after a successful pit stop, I could only assume Kathi was right.

One night he woke for the first pit stop right on schedule. I jumped up, eager to see if I could set a new record. He was screaming louder and harder than normal as I quickly laid him down to get to work mixing his formula with water. I was going as fast as I could, but I could not figure out what he was so upset about. I reached for the back of his head in an attempt to comfort him and felt something hard, about the size of my fist, attached to the back of his head.

At less than a year old Quinn had a lot of hair. It was the kind of big Afro that went out of style with disco. His hairstyle was something between Don King and the character Link from the 1970's TV show, *The Mod Squad*. I tried to figure out what was stuck to his head while still staying on pace for a record-setting pit stop. Whatever it was, Quinn didn't like it being there, a fact he had communicated by then to the entire neighborhood. The shape was that of a shoe with straps -- he had a sandal stuck to his head!

Someone, probably our nanny, had for an unknown reason left one of his sandals -- with a Velcro strap open -- lying in his crib. Quinn must have rolled over onto it and now the Velcro strap was firmly attached to his frizzy head of hair. I found out right away the hookup between Velcro and Afro forms a bond stronger than super glue. Any chance for a record-setting time was out the window. This pit stop had a major complication.

Mad at myself for being overconfident and putting the flashlight back in the garage, I had to operate in complete darkness as I delicately tried to remove the Velcro strap from the back of his head. It must have hurt because he did not stop screaming. In his hysteria he kicked the open formula bottle out of my other hand, sending warm water and undissolved powder all over the front of him and forming a gooey mess.

I quickly reviewed my situation. I had a hungry baby who was now soaking wet and with a sticky substance covering much of his body. The Velcro strap was still stuck in his hair. I couldn't see a damn thing. Complicating everything was the scent of a very dirty diaper. It was time to break the rules.

I flipped on the lights, and contrary to Kathi's opinion, Quinn's nervous system only alerted him to close his eyes. He also stopped crying. Now that things had calmed down considerably I found a pair of scissors to cut the sandal out of his hair. A couple of snips and the catastrophe was over. I started the pit stop over with a new bottle and a clean diaper. I kept the lights on and he kept his eyes closed. When I was done Quinn went back to sleep a lot faster than I did. Before I went back to bed I wrote a note and stuck it to his crib "do not leave shoes in this crib…or else."

As I drifted back to sleep I thought about how the kids had been with us in their new home for nine days, and how they were starting to settle into their surroundings and routine. Day by day their frantic need for our attention had given way to a growing sense of relaxed confidence. They had started pitching in with preparing meals and doing chores around the house. Amelec was already becoming more proficient than I at operating the TV remote control. It was comforting to observe their transformation, but, on the next morning, Day 10, things were going to get very complicated. It would be their first day at school.

We had identified one of the finest private schools in the Phoenix area and Kathi had lobbied hard enough that both Amelec and Espie had been accepted and admitted months ago. We could only imagine what a convoluted and demanding challenge the first six months of school would be for anyone in their circumstance, so our strategy had been to find an environment that would be supportive of their unique needs. Anyway you cut it, it was not going to be easy for them. They were going to be two black kids in a basically all-white school, they didn't speak English, and culturally they had not been exposed to any of the Hannah Montana-social trappings of their generation. They were from Haiti, but they just as easily could have been from Mars.

The school year in Arizona started early, about the second week in August, and this particular school had started two weeks ago. The previous week we had driven them over to the school in an effort to prepare them for what they were in for. The principal greeted Amelec and Espie with open arms and gave them an extensive tour of the place. The kids also had the opportunity to meet briefly with the teachers they were going to have. During the tour I remembered back to a time in my own youth when I had to change schools during the middle of the year. Joining and integrating into an already functioning group was hard for me. I remembered how much of an outsider I was, and how alone I felt when I was ushered into the classroom and all eyes turned to stare at the new kid. I could empathize to a degree with what our kids were about to go through. I was more worried than excited for them. I did not want our kids to have to eat lunch by themselves on their first day of school.

El Dorado school had a great reputation, and I was amazed Kathi was able to get our kids accepted into the program in the first place. The school's web page described its lofty goals and values: to offer an advanced educational curriculum and promote students to a higher academic level. The web page also said the school's "hands-on, minds-on activities bring students to high levels of thinking and application." It sure seemed like a very advanced place, beyond the range of any learning environment in Haiti. It was probably light years ahead of the grammar school I went to as well. I reviewed the web page one more time before I went to bed that night and I wondered if it was going to be too much. I wondered whether we had made another rookie parenting mistake.

The Monday morning reality arrived on schedule. El Dorado's parenting handbook, which was a great resource that gave us some solid advice, advised us to get the kids up in plenty of time to get them ready and to get a good breakfast into them. The handbook also said dealing with the combination of separation and adjustment to a new environment was going to be hard on the kids. It could also be hard on the parents, the book said. It encouraged us to "Smile and act confident the morning of the first day of school, because a parent's body language will say more than words." It was a stretch for me to act confident that morning, because I doubted my own judgment. A big part of me said we were moving too fast and rushing our kids into this. On top of that, I knew how cruel kids can be, another thing I was worried our children would have to face.

During breakfast I kept thinking to myself "maybe we should call this off." Maybe we should have someone come to school them at home, work with them for a year, let them learn the language and let them gently develop. There was so much they did not know, and so much they could not say. It did not even seem fair. How would they get by? Kathi and I had done a fair share of research on this, and of course everyone had a different opinion. I took a deep breath, put the dishes in the sink, wiped the kids' faces, and loaded them into the car. Some of the expert advice we had heard said to throw them in feet first and we would be amazed at how resilient they were. That's exactly what we were about to do.

The handbook said that on the first day it would be best if we dropped them off and then ran away. It didn't use those exact words, but it did say the first day would be emotional for everyone and the best way to handle the stress was to "get your child to their classroom, quickly say goodbye, and NOT LINGER!" That made a lot of sense to me, because I was never good at lingering, anyway. We parked the car, straightened out their brand new uniforms and put their backpacks on. Surprisingly, they did not look scared, they looked proud, like soldiers marching in a parade. They filed right in line with us as we headed for Espie's Pre-K classroom. I did my part: I smiled and acted confident. The teacher opened the door, welcomed Espie, and told us it was time to say goodbye. I could tell there was a sense of urgency in the teacher's tone, so we gave Espie an abbreviated hug and quick kiss before the door closed. Our daughter was in school. It had all happened so quickly. We hadn't even had a chance to linger.

Now it was Amelec's turn, and since he had just witnessed the orderly way Espie had entered her classroom, he was all business, and he was certainly not going to show any emotion or fear. In fact Kathi tried to hold his hand as we walked down the hall to his classroom and he wanted nothing to do with that. I suppose that was his way of demonstrating his manhood and I said to myself "good for him." There were a few other kids saying goodbye at the door of Room 7, Amelec's kindergarten class, and while others were milling around we brought him over to his teacher and reintroduced him. Amelec looked at me as if to say, "You're done, get out of here, I will be fine." We gave him a high five and we left.

Kathi and I walked down the hall in shock. It had been too easy; it almost did not seem real. Both Espie and Amelec appeared not only to understand what was happening, they embraced it. They seemed to enjoy being there, with their uniforms, backpacks, and supplies, in the midst of other kids. Then it dawned on me. They had not been around other kids since they had been home. Their previous life at the orphanage was defined by constantly being part of a pack of kids. No wonder they almost seemed glad to get rid of us.

However, as we walked down the hallway to the parking lot, I knew it would not be that easy. Their comfort in being around other children would soon be overtaken by the multitude of challenges they were going to face. In six hours we would be picking them up in the Grand Touring Experience, and then we would have our first indication of how resilient they really were. We would know whether throwing them in feet first was the right thing to do. Before we got to the parking lot, I took a quick detour to sneak a peek through the window of Espie's classroom, just to see if she was OK. Even though no one could see me peering through the corner of the window, I was in direct violation of the "No Lingering" rule.

To hell with it, I had to know.

* * *

Later, at the end of the school day, we were so excited to see how the kids had done we arrived back at El Dorado a half hour early, which meant I was violating the lingering rule again. Kathi and I had spent the entire day wondering how they were doing. I had hoped for the best and expected the worst, but it was fun to speculate, especially based on how surprisingly well the drop-off had gone. Thirty minutes in a parking lot is a long time, enough time to consider 101 outcomes. Finally the gates opened and we were free to go get them.

Kathi and I split up at the gates, with Kathi going to Amelec's classroom and I going after Espie. I don't know why I was expecting so much more drama, but when I hustled over to the Pre-K room, Espie seemed, well, fine. She was standing in line like the other kids, and she broke into a smile when she saw me. I quickly scanned for any visual signs of trauma. Nothing there; all systems were go. But now it was time to drill down and find out what really happened.

I made a beeline to the teacher and eagerly asked, "How did my little girl do?"

"She did great!"

"Really?"

"Uh, yes, really."

The teacher left me and began scurrying about, herding her students into the departure line, making sure children and stuff matched up. The end of the day was a hectic time, and I could understand why I did not receive much detailed information. Still, I wanted more. "She did great" was a rather generic response, and I did not know if I should believe it. I decided to take it to the source. I knelt down in front of Espie, looked her in the eye, and said, "How did you do, honey?"

She just smiled and said, "Good."

OK, I certainly wasn't getting overloaded with

information here. I looked around to see if anyone in the room could help me out, but everyone was preoccupied with their own challenges of finding the corresponding lunch pails and backpacks. It was only the first day for Espie; the rest of the kids had been in class for some two weeks, enough time to build up a sizable lunch pail supply in the lost and found.

So I did what a dad should do. I gave her a big hug and told her I was proud of her. Espie and I sauntered down the hall and out the doors of the school, meeting Amelec and Kathi back at the car. The four of us had one big group hug by the side of the car. Whatever had really happened, it was over, and we had made it through the first day of school. Neither of the kids was traumatized or upset; in fact they seemed pretty matter-of-fact about the whole experience, so I felt safe assuming on balance the day went well.

Based on that assumption it was time to celebrate, or play, or do something fun. When we got home, we gave the kids a snack and I plopped them down in the beanbag chairs in front of the TV so they could relax and unwind for a few minutes. I left the room to talk with Kathi to figure out what we should do to celebrate and when I returned, both of them were slumped into the beanbag chairs, sound asleep. They were deeply out. I imagined that with all the thinking they had done in school, by the end of the day their circuits must have been overloaded. I quietly turned the TV off and covered them up as they slept it off.

Since the drop-off went so well the first day, Kathi and I decided we would take turns dropping off and picking up, so one of us could do something else on their off day.

I volunteered to go first and take tomorrow. I certainly wasn't worried about flying solo. In fact I thought I would ramp things up a bit and take Quinn with me. I was anxious to show him the school he would someday be attending. Another reason I looked forward to the morning was that it would be my first trip out by myself as a dad with all three kids.

"You're sure you don't want to take a stroller for Quinn?" Kathi asked me for the third time as the kids were getting in the car the next morning.

"What do I need a stroller for? I'm going to carry him. Kath, I am only going to be at school a few minutes. My goodness, let's not make things harder than they need to be. In the time I would take to expand the stroller, strap him in it, and deal with all of those procedures, I could easily carry him around as I take the kids to their classrooms. This is no big deal; they did great yesterday. I'll be back in 20 minutes."

We got a front row spot to park in and as the kids got out of the car they did not have the same spring in their step as yesterday. I unstrapped Quinn from his car seat and shouldered him into one arm, while my other arm helped Amelec and Espie into their backpacks. The proud soldier look of yesterday had vanished from their faces. It had been replaced by something resembling the look of a 50-year-old man right before his first proctology exam.

"Come on guys!" I said. "What's wrong? Hey …we are back at school! This is going to be fun …You get to see all of your buddies again … Come on! let's march!" I tried to recreate some of yesterday's positive energy.

In response, Amelec and Espie dragged themselves through the gates and limped down the halls. As we arrived at the door of the Pre-K classroom, Espie looked up at me with those puppy dog eyes as if to say, "Dad, do I have to?" I knelt down and gave her a one-armed hug since my other arm was wrapped around Quinn, who was beginning to fuss. Espie did cheer up a bit when she saw her teacher and some of the other kids, and with an escalating enthusiasm she waved good-bye and went into her classroom.

"Come on Amelec, your turn," I said, remembering the advice from the handbook to act confident and smile. Quinn was becoming slightly agitated and could not seem to get comfortable in the way I was holding him. Amelec did not look so good either as we approached his classroom. The open-air hallway was packed with young kids scurrying about with their young moms. In the midst of the flurry of traffic, I noticed I was the only man in the hallway, and I felt like the oldest person in the zip code by at least one generation. I am sure I stood out as the token grandpa bringing his grandson to school and toting around an 11-month-old baby who was giving off the impression he did not want to be carried around anymore, accentuated by the fact our skin colors did not match.

I started gently pulling Amelec down the hallway because he had downshifted into slow motion. Ultra slow motion. As we hit the spot that would have marked the center of the hallway, which was also the busiest portion of the entire school, Amelec let go of my grip and fell to the ground like a sack of potatoes. As he lay at my feet, crying hysterically, I took it as a sign the first day of school had not gone as well as we'd thought.

# Chapter 14

## Cellophane Surprise

In harmony with his older brother's thunderous meltdown, Quinn began to wail. I realized the stroller would have come in pretty handy right about then.

I tried to pick Amelec up with one arm while hanging on to a squirming 11-month old in the other. Amelec weighed close to 40 pounds, but in his limp and motionless state he seemed to weigh about 100 pounds. In other words, unless I was able to quickly locate a crane, he was going to be darn near impossible to pick up.

Then something wonderful happened. One of the attractive young moms came to my rescue, smiled, and simply said, "Don't feel bad, we have all been there." Then, in the movements of an angel, she gently reached out and took Quinn from me so I could use both hands to pick up the sobbing sack of potatoes still lying on the floor. Once I had him in my arms Amelec caught his breath and calmed down a bit. The angel said to me in a calm voice, "Why don't I walk you down to where the school counselor is. You guys can all hang out there for a little while."

Her voice was so soothing, and who was I to ask questions? I was just so appreciative of the help. The young woman had brought an end to the whole chaotic moment, and a serene mood prevailed. She was so different from me, so in control and relaxed. I wondered, "Wow, is this what an expert parent looks like?" Quietly I followed her with Amelec as she led the way to the counselor's office with Quinn in her arms. When we got there, she handed Quinn over and before I could say thanks, she vanished.

The counselor was very helpful and quickly restored Amelec's composure. We hung out for a half hour or so until the counselor told me I should "probably go ahead and leave" and that she would make sure Amelec safely joined his classmates. In truth I was getting anxious to leave; after lugging Quinn around for the last hour he was getting heavy. I said goodbye to Amelec and he seemed like he had returned to normal as he gave me a big hug. I wasn't too worried as I was very impressed with how the school had handled the situation. They clearly knew what they were doing, and since I clearly didn't, it was probably just as well I got out of there. I put Quinn back in his car seat and made a note to myself to make a permanent storage spot in the car for his stroller.

When I got home I had some explaining to do to Kathi, and of course I had to hear about the umpteen reasons why you "always take a stroller with you." I also called the school counselor to check in. She had assured me that "while Amelec's meltdown may have seemed severe," she said that she didn't view it as abnormal behavior for a child in his circumstance. I appreciated her assurances, but no matter what she said I could hardly classify what happened in the hallway this morning as normal. Anyway it looked like the episode was behind us and the good news was I was not going to have to deal with it for a while. Kathi had the next drop-off and pick-up.

The one thing I am beginning to learn in the early stages of parenthood is that it is always one thing after another. The most recent stress was the first few days of school, but that was yesterday's news and the next day had its own tensions in store: We were scheduled to take all three kids to the doctor.

The kids had been tested for communicable diseases and had been checked out medically prior to final approval for the adoptions. Because of that we felt confident our kids were at least reasonably healthy, but we wanted our new pediatrician to take a look under their hoods just to validate -- or invalidate -- that belief.

When Gina and I found Quinn, there was a high probability he would test positive for HIV. I didn't know what the actual statistics were, but it was a safe bet most babies abandoned on the streets of Port-Au-Prince would turn out to have HIV or some other communicable disease. But Quinn was clean. He had been tested twice, as had all of the kids at the crèche, his good test results yet another example of how he beat the odds.

While all three kids had received their sequence of vaccines in Haiti, our pediatrician advised us to go ahead and administer the necessary vaccines here in the States just to make sure. Kathi and I agreed -- we had seen firsthand how incompletely many tasks were performed in Haiti.

So that meant our kids were going to get not only their first U.S. examinations and blood work, they were going to get shots, which meant needles, which meant Kathi was going to have to opt out of this doctor's visit. I was a little nervous to go out again on my own with the kids, especially since the first attempt at it had not gone so well. But we had found a terrific young pediatrician who had an excellent reputation. That gave me something to bank on. I had called ahead to see if I could bring all three of them in at once, a team visit.

Dr. Engle met us in the exam room, joined by a nurse who had all kinds of stuff on a tray. With the four of us and the two of them it was a bit crowded in the small room. We spent a few minutes getting acquainted, and then Dr. Engle spelled out what would happen during the visit. There would be blood draws from each of the kids for the lab work. That would be followed by a physical exam, and then each kid would get their own series of vaccines, which would vary from kid to kid. After a little bit of thought we decided to create an assembly line, rotating the three of them in a sequence of blood draw, physical exam and then shots. My job was to hold each of them down any time a needle was going to enter their skin.

Quinn being the smallest, he was first in line. I stood him up on the table, and as I undressed him for the examination, he peed all over the front of me the instant I took his diaper off. Clearly a method of primal communication. Doctor Engle and her nurse Nancy -- beyond doubt experts in dealing with kids -- told me babies pee on their parents all the time. That was interesting news, but it didn't dry my shirt. It was great to see how well Dr. Engle and Nancy got along with the children, and they made a very thorough visit fun for the kids, not counting the needle part. And other than having pee all over my shirt and having all three of them whimper and squirm when they had needles stuck in them, the visit exceeded my expectations. Dr. Engle said all three kids looked very healthy, and we would get a full report in a few days once the blood work was finished.

Things were going much better than the day before at school, and I was anxious to get on my way while I was ahead. I stood up and said, "Well that was great!" and I told the kids it was time to head home when Dr. Engle interrupted me.

"Well, there is one more thing we have to cover with you," she said. "There's going to be a little homework assignment. Here are 15 vials -- we need you to put 5 stool samples from each of them in these vials."

"Um, you mean … collect their poop?"

"Well, unfortunately, yes."

"How much ... I mean ... how do I … well with Quinn and his diapers I can see … I can see that could be done fairly easy … at least I think it will be … but … but how ... what about ... how do I collect ...?"

I stopped stammering. I asked nurse Nancy if she would be kind enough to take the kids out of the exam room for a minute so I could talk with Dr. Engle alone. She whisked them out of the room as if she had expected my request.

"Doc … do I really have to do this? What I mean is,

how do I do this?"

"Cellophane."

"What?"

"You put cellophane over the toilet. Not on the seat, but between the seat and the bowl. The trick is to seal the toilet and not tell the children. Then when they go, the cellophane catches the poop. It's pretty easy, actually."

"Easy?" I stared at her in disbelief. "Doc, I don't want to be disrespectful, catching our kids' poop in a toilet rigged with cellophane may sound easy to you, but, well, there is something you need to know about me. I gag pretty easily."

She laughed. I wasn't kidding.

"What do I do with it once it is in the cellophane?"

She held up one of the vials as if it was some sort of door prize. "See these? You need a tablespoon from each collection in each vial, and you need all five vials for each child completed within a 10-day period."

"What do I do with it once I get it into the vial?"

"You store it in the refrigerator until you bring it to the lab."

I stared into space. The refrigerator? Tablespoons? There were too many inferences to kitchen things for my liking. Talk about being blindsided. I was astounded.

But I had also heard enough, and like a coach who is arguing with a referee, 99 percent of the time it is a waste of time. So I surrendered. I was going to have to spoon poop into a plastic container and then store it in our fridge. None of the adoption counselors ever mentioned anything like this. Someone should have given me a heads-up.

She reached out to hand me the bag of vials and I

reluctantly took them, as if by accepting them, I was entering into a contract and had agreed to actually do it. I was shell-shocked as I came out of the room. The kids were happy to see me and they gave me a big hug. I think they thought I was in there getting my shots and they were trying to comfort me. I took all of the comfort they could give me as we walked on out to the car.

There comes a time in a guy's life when enough is enough and he has to draw the line. As I walked out of the doctor's office, I knew my time to draw the line had come. Look, I was more than willing to get up with Quinn at all hours of the night, more than happy to have the birds-and-bees discussion down the road, and fine with shampooing puke out of a carpet, but as far as collecting poop from a cellophane-tricked-up toilet ... no way. I was going to have to exercise some executive powers and assign that duty to someone else.

Kathi.

The good news is we got our lab reports back and the kids' blood work was fine. Amazingly, Quinn's blood work was off-the-charts. Turns out he was radically healthy, and from that point forward Dr. Engle started referring to him as the miracle baby. When you think about his beginnings, the odds of his having a dreadful disease were far greater than the odds of his being off-the-charts healthy. We were delighted with this news.

I was almost equally delighted Kathi had agreed to take on the poop collection detail. Practically, it was her way of saying that if she didn't handle it, it would never get done.

While we are on the subject, after the first eventful week of school, Kathi, intent on reinforcing all of the progress we were making, decided Amelec needed a belt to go around his pants. Amelec was 5 and in kindergarten, but had never worn a belt. At first the belt was a big hit with Amelec, and the first morning he wore it he strutted around the kitchen before breakfast showing it off like a runway model displaying the latest fashion. It was harmless fun until we received a call from the school around noon.

"Mr. Juntunen, this is Ms. Easton from El Dorado private school. We have had a little accident."

My heart dropped, imagining one of the kids had broken a leg or worse. "What's wrong?"

"Well, Amelec had a little accident. Don't get alarmed -- what happened is that he had to go to the bathroom and he didn't quite make it. I can't exactly understand what he is trying to say to me, because right now he is pretty upset. But what I think he is trying to say is that he could not get his pants down ... Does that make any sense to you?"

"Couldn't get his pants down? What? That can't be it … tell me again what he tried to say to you."

"Well, he keeps pointing at his belt or his zipper and he is ... I still can't understand ..."

"Oh -- Oh, he's pointing to his belt?"

"Yes, he is pointing to his belt, but he is crying, so …"

"Well, I think I know what happened. Kathi had given him a belt for his uniform today and he had never had a belt before. I bet she didn't show him how to unhook it. The poor kid ended up going in his pants, simply because he did not know how to get the belt undone."

"I think that is exactly what has happened here."

I told the superintendent to have everyone sit tight

and we would be right over. I shouted out to Kathi. "Honey, we have to take a fresh set of clothes to school for Amelec, and the clothes he is wearing may be ruined. That's the bad news. The good news is you won't need any cellophane for your first poop collection."

For the record Kathi swore the poop collection activity was the worst thing she ever had to do in her life, and nothing humanly imaginable will ever surpass it. I will have to take her word for it. My participation in the activity was virtually untraceable. I did not even open the refrigerator for nine days. When one of the kids went to use a toilet covered with cellophane, I managed to excuse myself to attend to some sort of "emergency cleanup" around the pool or in the yard. After those nine days our pool was the cleanest it had ever been.

When the poop collection and testing were done, we learned that Espie had some kind of parasite which was very common in children from Haiti and which was easily flushed out of her system with antibiotics. In retrospect, it might have been just as easy to assume all three had the parasite, sparing Kathi a lot of grief and several rolls of cellophane. Of course under that scenario the pool would not have been as clean.

Looking back on this period it would be easy to criticize Kathi and me for doing too much with the kids. In hindsight we were overloading them -- and ourselves. I suppose we were just anxious to show them the kind of life we wanted to offer them, and since there were so many things available to our kids, we kind of got carried away. A week after they started school we signed them up for karate lessons. It was a really great program, designed to teach kids valuable life and character lessons.

The owner of the business was also the teacher and he was spectacular. The problem was that in addition to the karate moves, there was a significant listening portion in which the teacher would tie the moves and the character values together. As a parent I thought this was the best part. But our kids didn't understand a word he was saying, so those moments were boring for them. Our kids did the moves very well, and it was astounding to see how athletic they were. They would watch the teacher demonstrate a move, stand at the back of the line so they could see other kids do them first, then imitate what they had seen. Although I was impressed with their resourcefulness, the fact they couldn't understand what the teacher was saying underscored for me how unbelievably difficult school must be for them. How in the world were they keeping up in the classroom? Watching the karate classes gave me a tremendous appreciation for how demanding their lives were.

Clearly, for all of us, there had been a dramatic shift in our lifestyle. The change was extreme. Since Quinn had arrived as the third body in our bedroom I was getting up two or three times a night. Even when Kathi was getting up with him, I was still waking up, and I had a hard time falling back to sleep in either case. I would describe my condition as sleep-deprived, especially in comparison to how well I had slept in the previous 51 years of my life.

One day before I had to pick up the big kids at school, I met a friend for an early lunch and a quick nine holes of golf. He hadn't seen me since the kids had come home, and he of course wanted to know how things were going. I gave him a few highlights, like the night the sandal got stuck in Quinn's hair. He told me he thought I looked

162

tired. I told him he was wrong -- I was exhausted. We started talking about Quinn, what it was like to have his crib in our room, and babies in general. Then he told me something that added a new worry to my life. He told me about a friend of his whose baby slept in a crib in the master bedroom, just like Kathi and I were doing with Quinn. And then one morning the friend got up to find his baby had died of sudden infant death syndrome.

I sat motionless as my friend continued the story, and how his buddy entered a living hell. Not only was his son gone, which had to be the worst thing anyone could experience, but there was also a police investigation and a coroner report that followed the tragedy. It was one of the worst stories I had ever heard. Our kids had not been home for long, but I was very attached to them and couldn't imagine how painful it would be if something happened to them. To think of waking up one morning and finding Quinn gone was beyond my comprehension. I had heard of SIDS before, but it had just seemed like something horrible that happened to somebody else. Now it was a possibility in my own life. I was beside myself.

I couldn't say anything to Kathi about it for a few days; I didn't want to scare her the way I had been scared. Before I heard the story at lunch my state was sleep-deprived. From then on it would be very sleep-deprived, mortified, and obsessed with stopping SIDS from happening to us. After that, in addition to the regular Quinn pit stops, I also woke up many other times in the night just to check on him. It especially worried me that no one knows why or how SIDS happens. I hated the feeling of not being in control, which, unfortunately, is a big part of parenting. You give your all so your kids will have the best opportunities and chances in life, but there will always be things that are beyond your control. I had a hard time accepting that randomness. For the next several months I got up an extra few times a night just to make sure my precious Quinn was still breathing.

# Chapter 15

## Both Ends Burning

"Man must feel the earth to know himself and recognize his values. God made life simple. It is man who complicates it." -- Charles Lindbergh.

In an earlier portion of my life I used to receive a series of cortisone shots in my elbow. Before the injections the doctor would say, "This is going to hurt a little." The problem with that communication was that "hurt" and "little" are relative terms. And as far as I was concerned those shots hurt a lot more than a little. When I mentioned to a friend who was an experienced father that we were going to bring home three kids under the age of 5 from Haiti, that friend told me "your life is going to get a lot more complicated." "A lot more" and "complicated" are also relative terms. It turned out he was very right. I had no idea how complicated "complicated" could be.

A small campfire is just a breath of wind away from burning a forest down. Fueled by the best of intentions, our friends and relatives wanted to show support for our bringing the kids home from Haiti. Their support manifested itself in the form of delivering gifts. It started out as a few simple and generous gestures, but the winds started to pick up, and soon the entire forest was ablaze. It was natural to have our friends want to meet our kids, and when they came over to meet them, they brought gifts for them. But people whom I might describe as acquaintances and some whom I barely knew started ringing the bell and dropping off gifts and a welcome note on the front door step. The word had gotten out we had adopted three kids from the poorest country in the Western Hemisphere, and it seemed as if every current or past member of our Christmas card list wanted to make sure the children knew they were welcome in our country. Despite our continued pleas to not do so, many wonderful and generous people gave, delivered, or sent cards and gifts, more than I could count.

Complaining about the generosity of our friends and our relatives may seem ungrateful. But our kids' expectations of their new life, in this new place, were being shaped and transformed minute to minute. With a daily barrage of gift-wrapped boxes for them to open, it was only natural for them to acquire a huge misunderstanding. This circumstance was not normal to everyday life, but since it had been happening nearly from the first day they had arrived, it sure seemed normal to them. We could see what was happening, and we knew how these kind acts could warp their perspective. We wanted our kids to get off to a grounded and humble start in their new life. But as they were getting showered with cards and gifts, they took what was happening at face value: "This is the American way, and it's a heck of a lot better than Haiti." Explaining it all to them was going to be complicated enough, but the fact they could understand very little of what we would try to say made it even more complicated.

At the very beginning of the landslide of gifts, we felt we were between a rock and a hard place as the early visitors were our good friends and we did not want to hurt their feelings. But once we saw the potential damage the runaway gift train could do to our children, we started telling our friends that, while we wanted you to come meet the kids, please don't bring any gifts. Simple enough, but here's what we were up against. We have a lot of friends who have been very successful, and with all of that success, they don't necessarily think certain rules and requests apply to them.

We continually sent out the message not to send or bring gifts, sometimes even adding the message: "Gifts might be a negative for our kids at this early stage." But the recipients of those messages viewed them as meant for someone other than themselves. As ridiculous as it may seem, the runaway train got so far down the tracks we could no longer manage our own family.

This whole fiasco was a very interesting experience because what we were saying apparently did not seem to resonate with anyone. Despite what we thought were clear instructions, the gifts kept showing up in rapid fire order from our friends and family and all we could do was continue to be appreciative and grateful and manage the predicament as gracefully as we could. But in the avalanche of gifts, our kids' perspectives and expectations were running amok. One time a friend showed up to say hello, thankfully without gifts in hand, and our kids thought some how a mistake had been made.

To bellyache about it may have seemed absurd, and I can only imagine how awful it sounded for me to gripe. But the more it continued the more I wanted it to stop. Trying to explain my viewpoint was, well, complicated. We tried to be grateful, and we wished we had had the tools to manage the gift-giving differently. But once the fire got started, it raged beyond our control. It wasn't long before our garage started to look like a department store, and eventually our kids became numb to everyone's generosity, as opening one present after another started losing its meaning.

With our kids now believing that they were the grand prizewinners in the *Toys R Us* sweepstakes, Kathi and I had differing views on how we should have dealt with it in the first place. Then we disagreed on what to do with all the gifts. Philosophical disagreements between Kathi and I were becoming more commonplace. In fact it was becoming apparent Kathi and I had two very different parenting philosophies. She and I had been together for a long time, and in that time we had always seen just about everything eye to eye. When it was just us and all we did was ski and golf there really wasn't much to disagree about. But as parents, we were as different as Republicans and Democrats.

My parenting style was closer to that of Vince Lombardi and her parenting style was closer to that of Mary Poppins. She wanted to make things comfortable and easy for the kids, and I wanted to toughen them up.

Kathi is one of the nicest people on the planet, and of course I am not one of the nicest people on the planet. Kathi was one who always was doing things for others, always volunteering for extra duty in whatever club or organization she was part of. She was the one who would gladly do the job no one else wanted to do. And she hates to say no. I love her for her generosity and selflessness, but when it comes to children, I think saying no must be a critical, active component in the parenting tool box. Otherwise kids begin to acquire an entitlement mentality and start believing the world owes them something.

The one thing that was crystal clear to me was the parents are the parents, and are therefore in charge. Kids are kids and are not in charge. I have seen that this perspective is not crystal clear to other parents, including, at times, my wife. What I see now and again is parents who are intimidated by their kids, and the parents end up accommodating, coddling and babying their kids. Instead of parents telling their kids what to do, I see them in negotiations with their kids in an effort to get them to behave. Kathi believed this to be a more sophisticated and contemporary parenting style that evolved through the benefit of expert analysis and research. I saw such New Age parenting as very different from how I was brought up, and I believed New Age parenting could put our country at risk of raising a generation of spoiled brats.

When we started out as parents, Kathi was surprised to learn how old-fashioned I was. It was a side of me she had not seen before. Unlike Kathi, I had no problem saying no. I also believed in tough love, and that characteristics like discipline, mental toughness, and a threshold of pain can and must be taught to kids so they can grow up prepared to compete within the cruel realties of the world. I am old school and Kathi is contemporary, which interestingly enough, after all of these years, was news to our relationship. It netted out that at times she was too accommodating and I was too demanding. At times, these conflicting styles made things a bit confusing for our kids, and it made our lives, well, a little more complicated.

The good news was Kathi and I benefitted from having always been a great team, able to flow with each other as various phases in our lives came and went. As our parenting years add up I am sure she will drift a little over to the old school and I will drift a little toward the contemporary way of thinking. Meanwhile our philosophies will complement each other, and our kids will benefit from the yin and yang. There will be disagreements, as she will always want to give them two popsicles for dessert and I will only want to give them one, if any. I had to accept that our kids' mom had a very different parenting style from my own, which made things more complicated, but not impossible.

As our kids started to understand and speak English, watching TV was another thing that became more complicated. One afternoon I sat down to watch a football game with Amelec, a little father and son bonding, a time to share with him the great American game. The game was fine, but the commercials killed the experience. He pointed to the screen and asked me all kinds of questions. Not about the football game, but about Viagra, and beer, and a drug for shrinking your prostate. The worst commercial was an advertisement for a video game that had violent and scary content. Of course Amelec wanted to know all about the video game, and in broken English asked if we had one. I asked myself "Don't these TV executives have kids?" I became so disgusted with the things we were being force-fed on the commercial breaks I punched the remote and we watched cartoons on the Disney channel instead.

Video games represent another pending dimension to the complicated prism of contemporary parenting. I certainly don't want our kids becoming video game junkies, or junkies of any of the other things TV shows and media promote. I want our kids to be kids, which in my mind means to go out and play, building a fort or a tree house, playing ball with their friends for hours on end like I used to. I want our kids to learn how to become winners on the fields of competition and to succeed in the classroom. I don't want them sitting in a chair in front of a computer working their thumbs to kill off megapixel bad guys. Maybe this is similar to the gift situation, and there is not a whole hell of a lot I can do about it. Clearly being a kid today is different than when I was a kid. I am not sure how I am supposed to come to terms with that.

The kids came home on August 26. Christmas Day was quickly approaching, the 4-month anniversary of our becoming a family. Their transformation over the past four months had been remarkable. Their meltdowns were gone, their testing the boundaries of our relationship was done at least for now, and they had rapidly picked up bits and pieces of English. They were not fluent, but they were certainly conversational, and we could all roughly communicate with each other. That made things easier, but it also made things more complicated.

Quinn took his first steps and he was now walking.

We celebrated for a few hours and then realized how dramatic a change it represented, as he had become a moving target. Thereafter he required constant supervision -- if we took an eye off him for a minute, he was gone. Overnight his motor skills went from slow crawl to jackrabbit. He had evolved to become the poster boy for why they invented pool fences.

The big kids were speaking English and Quinn was walking, and that was how they would experience their first Christmas at home. Like all other firsts, there was some explaining to do to Espie and Amelec, both of whom were now 5. Christmas is a tricky thing to explain to wide-eyed 5-year-olds who had only just arrived in our culture four months ago. There are more than plenty of moving parts that make up the event. For starters you have Santa Claus, the elves, the flying reindeer, the big workshop facility at the North Pole, the mysterious chimney entrance, and on and on. And it gets a little more complicated still when you factor in the fistful of religious interpretations that have their own take on the holiday season. "Does Santa really come down the chimney, Poppa?" Was one of many on an endless list of questions challenging my ingenuity as the holiday season hurtled toward us.

I was torn on how to spin the concept of Santa Claus to our kids. We had formed building blocks in the previous four months as our family had bonded and grown, and the cornerstone of that growing bond was trust. In my mind, Santa presented a problem. On one hand I didn't want to betray our growing trust and lie to them, and on the other I wanted them to experience the magic of Christmas and what that meant to a five-year-old. The tradition of placing milk and cookies out by the tree on Christmas Eve is part of the childhood experience. But for two of our kids it would only be a few years, at most, before they figured out Santa Claus really doesn't come down the chimney. Since they were just beginning to trust us, I was concerned about the ramifications of their finding out we had misled them. We had put together our Juntunen family values and we frequently talked about them with our kids. These stated values were our important guiding principles as a family. The first value was to always tell the truth -- hence the dilemma with Santa Claus.

Now Kathi and I had already decided not to participate in the rituals of the Easter Bunny or the Tooth Fairy, for we saw those concepts simply as deceptions we would need to unwind in a year or two. For us it made perfect sense to not even get started with the Easter Bunny -- that decision was easy. But what to do with the shopping mall Santa Claus, and everything else that goes with the magic of the season? For the first time in my life, Christmas had become complicated.

Another complication that really bummed me out was our dogs, who for years had been nothing but comforting companions. First of all, Espie never warmed to them and there was always an awkward tension when she and the dogs were in the same room. Amelec and Quinn liked the dogs well enough, and that was great, but the dogs were aging rapidly, losing their senses, and becoming increasingly needy. As if we needed more needy bodies around the house! Poor Bubba was even losing some of his mental capacities and was starting to occasionally pee in the house. One day when I was reveling in the joy of watching Quinn take some early steps down the hallway, he slipped in a pool of pee that Bubba had left behind. The joy of a simple endearing moment had given way to the sorrow of Quinn falling, crying and then rolling around in a puddle of Bubba's pee.

I have always liked things to be simple and straightforward. Maybe that is another way of describing "old school." I have come to accept that life in general is not that way, but still, that is how I would like things to be. When Kathi and I were on our own, things pretty much were simple and straightforward. In those days I had a sense of freedom and spontaneity. I am also very fond of getting eight uninterrupted hours of sleep. In the first four months I did not have one uninterrupted night of sleep. Spontaneity and freedom are distant memories, and I don't know if I will ever see simple and straightforward again. My friend who had alerted me that things were going to get complicated sure knew what he was talking about. He had been where I was; in fact, he was one up on me, as there was a time in his life when he had four kids under the age of 5. During our discussion, he used a phrase to describe that period of his life.

"Craig, there were times when it felt like both ends were burning."

"What does that mean?" I asked.

"You'll find out my friend ... you will find out soon enough."

With the kids and Kathi in bed, I plopped myself down in front of the Christmas tree to have a nightcap by myself. I had found a quiet moment to think about what he meant. It was one week until Christmas and he was right, both ends were burning. The simple straightforward life I had known was gone, replaced by waves of confusion and complications. Now very little was easy -- even sitting down to watch a football game with my son was a mixed bag. The tranquil waters I had been sailing on for all these years had been stirred up by a perfect storm. It seemed as if I was drowning in a new and different storm everyday. The relationship with my wife was changing. The relationship with my dogs was changing. Relationships with family and friends were changing. My relationship with me had changed. Relationships, events, rituals, gifts, television, and now even Christmas were getting caught up in the confusion. Between the kids, the nanny, the constant flow of visiting family and friends, there had been more people in and around this house over the last four months than there had been over the last fourteen years. But that night, as I sat in front of the Christmas tree, drinking a glass of red wine, I may have felt as alone as I had ever felt.

I was accustomed to being in charge of things. In my earlier life I was a quarterback at different levels of competition for fourteen seasons. And when I owned my company I resided in the corner office, the place where the buck stopped. I spent most of my life being in charge, and now with all of these outside influences, I was not in charge. The mindset and expectations of our kids was being shaped minute-to-minute by a wide range of outside forces, and I was only part of that equation, a smaller part than I was used to being. That was the frustration. I thought I knew the right messages to be sending these kids, but they were receiving input and messages from other sources, many of which I believed to be wrong. As a rookie parent I was residing between doubt and frustration, because I couldn't control most of the influences that were touching them, influences that would ultimately shape and form who they became.

About halfway through the glass of wine I stopped feeling sorry for myself and realized there was a hidden beauty in all of this. I had received everything I had asked for. I craved to be back on the edge, in some form of action, challenged and tested; for you only really discover your core when things get complicated. Before this, I was halfway dead and buried. I needed this. I did not know it at the time, but both ends burning is exactly what I had ordered.

I wanted to do something significant, one thing with the rest of my life that really meant something. I didn't know if I had it in me, but if I did, I wanted to make a tangible contribution to someone's life. The fact that it was not easy, and all of the complicated dimensions that were forcing me to adapt and grow only meant I had put myself exactly in the place I wanted to be. During these first four months the hard parts far outnumbered the easy parts and the not-so-fun parts outnumbered the fun parts, but that equation was far more appealing than the mindless carousel of country club cocktail parties.

As the days closed in on Christmas, we had come up with a way to deal with the details. We communicated to the kids that the spirit of Christmas lives inside each of us and by believing in Santa Claus we are connecting to a spirit of the greater good that is at the core of the human condition. In our lifetimes we all have to come to terms with our own Santa Claus and what he means in our lives. I told the kids there was a lifelong connection between Santa Claus and giving, and a part of us should always engage in the spirit and joy of giving to others. The irony was, while I was tripping my way through this tongue-tied explanation, very little of which the kids understood anyway, I was the one who rediscovered Christmas. I was inspired by the simplicity and innocence of the children's reaction to all the hubbub of the season, and that is what reconnected me to the real meaning of the holiday.

Unfortunately, the gift pile under the tree kept growing and expanding. The friends and relatives were at it again. As I watched the presents swell from under the tree and out into the living room, I shook my head at the excess. Our house had become a daily stop on the UPS route. But I was proud of myself -- this time I tried not to get too upset about it. I also had a plan. The only sensible thing to do was to take a good portion of these gifts and give them to needy kids who might not otherwise have a Christmas. We had bought bikes for our kids, and as far as I was concerned, the bikes and a couple pairs of underwear and socks would have been plenty for them.

We found a great organization that would distribute gifts to families who had fallen on hard times, meaning some other kids would have a Merry Christmas. The crew even helped us clean out the garage as they also took many of the earlier gifts that had long been forgotten by our kids. We explained to the kids what we were doing as we watched the crew load up the truck. Amelec and Espie seemed to understand this gesture, and I think they even felt good about it. Over dinner we continued to talk about why some of our gifts were going to other kids. It was a great conversation that enabled us to live the Christmas spirit as a family. That was Christmas Eve.

The kids went off to bed. Now that there was enough space in the living room for me to actually get near the tree, I placed the bikes next to the few other presents we had retained. We couldn't wait to teach them how to ride their first bikes in the morning. Kathi and I lit a fire and had some dessert. This was more like it. We reminisced about how far the kids had come, and we marveled at the fact they had been in Haiti only four months earlier. They had learned a good portion of the English language. They had started going to school and had made some friends. They had learned how to work the TV better than me. Amelec even mastered how to unhook a belt.

They had begun to shape and form their own identities. Their lives had changed a heck of a lot more than mine had over the same time. Christmas morning they would wake up in a nice house, with running water and electricity. They would open a few presents and ride their new bikes. It would be their first real celebration of Christmas.

When we bought the bikes I had inquired about also installing training wheels on them. The owner of the shop told me training wheels were a mistake; kids will quickly learn how to ride a bike without them. With them, they would develop a false sense of security, and learning to balance and ride will be much more difficult in the long run. He told me to take the money I was planning to spend on the training wheels and buy helmets and elbow pads instead. They will fall, he said, and the best thing you can do was let them fall. For they would only need to fall a few times before they would be able to "feel it" -- riding a bike is all about feel. They can't get that feel if the training wheels are on. Give them a good push, and let them go.

The bike shop owner had not only given me a lesson on how to teach my kids to ride a bike … he was a messenger teaching me how to be a better dad. He was trying to tell me I was thinking too much and not feeling enough. Maybe as a parent I needed to take their training wheels off and let them go. Maybe I also needed to take my own training wheels off, let my knees and elbows get a little bloody … then, I could develop my own feel for parenting. Maybe being a great dad was simply all about feel. Maybe I was making this too complicated and as I thought about it I could imagine that someday I would look back on this time and say, "It was a good Christmas. I am really glad I didn't buy those training wheels."

# Chapter 16

## Learning to Believe

I have watched brilliant, multi-colored sunsets in the Sonoran desert and I have looked in awe at the magnificent peaks of the Colorado Rockies. I have been hypnotized by pounding waves sweeping the coastline of Big Sur. I have seen more than my share of the majestic beauty this world has to offer, but after this morning I don't think I have seen anything more magical than watching our kids learn to ride a bike.

It was a cool, crisp and very clear Christmas morning in Scottsdale. We lived on a street that usually had a nominal amount of traffic, and it was a good bet there wasn't going to be any this morning. I rolled Espie's, then Amelec's brand new Christmas presents out from under the tree and onto the street. Blue and pink two-wheelers, no training wheels. I strapped their helmets on and gave each of them a knock on the head, for luck, and to make sure that the helmet was on properly. I stepped over to straddle Amelec's bike. I stared each of them in the eye and said one word: "Watch."

Our kids had never ridden a bike before, and I doubt they had even seen anyone ride a bike before. If I, or they, were going to have success this morning, experience told me showing them what to do, rather than telling them, was my best way to get started. I gave a modest demonstration, riding Amelec's small blue bike around in miniature circles. I looked like a clown in the circus, as the bike was at least a half dozen sizes too small for me and I was forced to stand up to pedal to avoid hitting my chin with my knees. They didn't care; they were just anxious for me to finish my demonstration so they could give it a try. In no time both were saying, "My turn, Poppa, my turn."

I had never given a lesson on how to ride a bike, and all I had to go on was the advice the man at the store had offered. I decided to have Amelec go first. I put Amelec on the seat, held him upright while I placed his feet on the pedals and, slowly started moving him forward. I held him up gingerly so he could sense his balance. I started barely jogging so the bike would pick up a little speed. I did a quick inspection of his facial expression -- all systems seemed to be go -- so I gave him a big push and let him fly. I anxiously watched to see if he was going to, as the man in the store said, "Feel it."

Unfortunately the only thing he felt was the asphalt. He crash-landed in less than two seconds. His performance was similar to vintage footage you see of early airplane flights. Like many of those early disastrous aeronautic experiments, the end came very abruptly.

Amelec hit the ground hard, and the perfect metallic paint job on his bike was no longer perfect.

Amelec was either scared or hurt, probably both, and although he tried not to, he couldn't help himself from crying. As usual, I wasn't going to baby him. My reaction was to get him back up on the bike before he had a chance to think what had happened. Thinking eliminates any athlete's sense of "feel," and since I was trying to get him to find the feel, the last thing I wanted him doing was thinking.

I quickly dusted him off and straightened out the handlebars. I managed to get him back on the bike and upright, ready for his second attempt, even though he was still whimpering. Espie, who had been waiting patiently for her turn, witnessed Amelec's painful outcome, giving her plenty of time to think about things. Her eagerness meter had dropped considerably as she was shuffling her feet backwards, trying to distance herself from the scene and unhook the chinstrap on her helmet at the same time. Amelec had a painful look of doubt on his face, Espie was physically and emotionally retreating, and I was wondering how much those training wheels would have cost me.

But this was Christmas morning, which meant purchasing accessories was no longer an option. We would have to proceed with what we had. I gave Amelec a hug for encouragement, and asked if he was ready to try again. He gave me the thumbs-up sign whether he meant it or not. For his second launch, I calculated a need for greater initial velocity, so I ran with him a little farther, and I pushed him a little harder. I let go, and he was on his own, again, still a little wobbly, but surviving and maintaining an upright position. It looked like he was starting to get the feel. Of course, right about then I made the mistake of enthusiastically cheering him on, which proved to distract him. As he turned his head around to see what I was jabbering about, he lost control and swerved into a large jojoba bush. But this was a softer landing, a better outcome, and more importantly it was more than 100 feet from the launching pad.

Amelec's first flight blew up on launch, but his second attempt made it to into the atmosphere. I turned my head to look over at Espie; Amelec's limited success had brought her glow back, and at least for now she stopped fiddling with her chinstrap. As I was helping Amelec up out of the jojoba, I turned to her and said "Your turn, princess." Espie's first ride demonstrated she can be the opposite of Amelec. I followed the same jog-and-push launch protocol, and off she went. And she went and went. She rode her pink bike halfway down the street, amazingly, her very first time on a bike. It was only out of confusion or surprise that she hadn't fallen yet, but I had not told her how she was supposed to stop. She realized she eventually needed to stop, so she simply tipped over. Amelec and I ran down to her in jubilation and once we reached her we swapped high fives in abundance.

Espie had experienced instant success. But it also looked like she could become a one-hit wonder. Whereas Amelec showed improvement and steady progress with each new attempt, Espie's bike-riding abilities got worse as her attempts went on. He kept going farther, and she kept falling sooner. Their development paths sharply crisscrossed. Despite, or maybe because of the opposing trend lines, they both became more and more determined to succeed. I could see they were keeping score as they took turns falling and getting up. A new turn, and another outcome, seemed to fuel their dogged determination.

It only took a few hours to prove the man in the store right. There had been plenty of falls, and luckily more tears than blood spilled. The collateral damage was now the bikes weren't new anymore, and some of the native landscape along the side of the road had been forcefully rearranged or squished. But by lunchtime determination had prevailed, and our kids knew how to ride their bikes. The first few flights had been mostly modest failures, and while there were a few spectacular falls, both kids were gritty, and after every crash they regrouped and got back up. With a hearty resolve showing in their clenched teeth, it was only a matter of time before they did in fact find a way to "feel it."

That Christmas morning I believe I witnessed their greatest personal achievement so far in their lives. Amelec and Espie had both been in the orphanage before the age of 2, and although the orphanage was a clean and healthy place, there wasn't much opportunity for either one to experience any personal breakthroughs. The early struggles of the falling and getting back up again process resulted in a joyful and independent bike ride that could only be described as a breakthrough. Something new and wondrous was now part of their lives.

I saw when it happened. The beauty was in being there for that moment. Observing their faces lighting up once they got it was a sight I will never forget. They knew they had accomplished something, and they were beaming as if they had just conquered the world. While it was fun to share in the experience, they no longer needed me to prop them up. They were ready to fly solo.

I encouraged them to venture out and ride the loop around our block. While they no longer needed me to push-start their rides, I would continue to push them in all of their future activities to surpass what they perceive as their limitations. In this case they had proven themselves as capable bike pilots and as far as I was concerned they were ready to go into orbit. The journey around the block was a very gentle and easy ride, and I considered the safety aspects before I made my suggestion. But on a relative basis it would be a huge adventure for them, and that was the point. I wanted to reward their perseverance and determination by letting them venture out on their own. They had earned this chance. There were risks, as there are in most things in life. For a few minutes they were going to be out of sight, on the dark side, navigating entirely on their own without any supervision. As they took off, I looked at my watch, knowing that if they hadn't made it around in a while I was going to have to mount a search-and-rescue.

As I sat and waited for them, I considered what had just happened and how quickly they had learned a new skill. They had become proficient in only a few hours. In a way it all seemed very easy. Of course I was not the one who was all scraped up. It may have happened very quickly, but that morning they learned a valuable lesson of perseverance and determination. As they came back to the house, easily completing their first orbit, they stopped to check in with me, proud and accomplished, still beaming, and asked if they could do it again.

"Of course, just be careful."

And just like that they were gone.

That Christmas they had found something other than a bike under the tree. Amelec and Espie had discovered a pathway to confidence. They had started out tentative and wary about the bike lesson, and had ended up confident and daring, bold enough to go around the block by themselves. And they were going to need their newly-found confidence: Kathi and I had decided to enroll them into some competitive activities, maybe even before they were ready.

I had signed Amelec up to play Pee Wee football and Kathi had found a competitive dance company for Espie to join. Not to be left out, Quinn also began to participate in a toddler gymnastics program two days a week. There is a natural growth curve for every child who begins to compete, but our kids had an additional dimension to that growth curve. Not only did they have to learn to compete; they had to learn it in a brand new culture. A competitive culture.

I realized I had jumped the gun having Amelec play organized football. It was 8-man, full-contact Pee Wee football, really just a bunch of little kids running around, but it was still very competitive. Amelec's command of English was still weak, and he certainly did not understand the concept or the rules of the game of football. The team practiced two nights a week and played games on Saturday. He was one of the youngest, smallest and least informed players on his team. Everything about the football experience was a first for him and he grew with the experience of every practice and game. The youth sport experience is really driven by the quality of the coaching, and we were really lucky as

Amelec had very competent and compassionate coaches. He started out as the worst player on the team, but he played in all of the games and by the end of the season he even started a few games. He had held his own and his sense of confidence grew. Even when he wasn't sure what he was doing, or whether he was doing something "right," he did it the best he could.

Espie had immediate success as a dancer. Kathi had put her in three different types of dances, which true to our form was probably too much. Despite the demanding workload, Espie hung in there. As was the case with learning to ride a bike, Espie had a fast start, but faltered as the classes and months went on. After the first few lessons, she closed her ears, mistaking the early success as an indication dance was going to be easy. When she stopped listening, she stopped learning. Espie and Amelec had moments of greatness and moments of mediocrity, but they were integrating into their activities successfully, and that is what mattered.

The days of school, dance, football and gym seemed to run together. Soon it was going to be Kathi's birthday, her first birthday as a mom. To avoid having to go to the mall to buy her a gift, I did what I always do and took the easy way out. I decided we should take a trip somewhere as a family. I researched a couple of ideas and decided upon Disneyland. The first description I read about it was that it was "the happiest place on earth."

Who wouldn't want to go there?

Disneyland has been described as "a make-believe world that turns everyone into a kid again. A place where dreams come true." A place where parents and children could have fun together sounded perfect. Going there sure sounded a heck of a lot better than going to the mall to buy my wife a sweater.

There was one hitch with the idea of going to Disneyland: I hated going on amusement park rides. In fact, I really can't go on rides. It turns out I have what doctors call a very sensitive equilibrium, a fancy way of saying I get sick on roller coasters. It is actually worse than that. I have been known to get queasy on fast-moving elevators. So the ads about the happiest place on earth sounded great, but the happy feeling began to leave me when I started imagining climbing aboard anything that spins or goes up and down. Before I booked the trip I had a couple of things to consider. One, would the grandeur of the Disneyland experience be overwhelming for our kids, who just a few months ago were highly entertained by hot and cold running water? And two, would it put a damper on the trip if the kids saw their dad throw up all over Dumbo the Flying Elephant?

After some back-and-forth internal debate, inspired by a strong desire to avoid going to the mall, I gave Kathi a simple card for her birthday. Inside was a note that read, "Happy Birthday, 3 days in Disneyland. Love…. your old husband and your three young kids."

We had decided to take the kids out of school so we could enjoy the park during a week when it would be less crowded. That meant there would be smaller lines for all of the rides I did not want to go on. We arrived on a Tuesday, checked into a spectacular hotel, and hustled straight over to the entrance of Disneyland, Main Street USA. Now for the reality check: Although I had read all the stuff about Disneyland being the Happiest Place on Earth, and a Place Where Dreams Come True, the odds were just as good the trip could become a nightmare. Kathi and I were traveling with three young kids we were still having difficulty communicating with, and we were going to be hoofing around an unfamiliar amusement park, which would include the certainty that Quinn was going to be cranky at least five times a day. But despite the risks, it still looked better than a trip to the mall.

From Haiti to Disneyland. Could we have provided anything more extreme to these kids? Once we walked through the turnstiles, Amelec's and Espie's expanding vocabulary had somehow shrunk to only two words: SPACE MOUNTAIN. My guess is that they had learned about the roller coaster, probably from some diabolical insight provided by their mom, and once we set foot on the park grounds all I heard from them were those two dreadful, stomach-churning words. It was inevitable during the trip I was going to have to hop aboard that ride, I was just hoping to find a way to put it off so I could warm up my touchy equilibrium on some gentle, slow moving rides.

There is a thin line separating the desire not to disappoint your kids and the desire not to throw up in public. Part of the parenting oath includes something like, "From this point forward your kids come first," which meant I should probably alert maintenance to meet us over at Space Mountain with some mops and a bucket. Along our route to the roller coaster were millions of potential diversions that could have saved me, but our kids were not biting. As if drawn by a magnet, Amelec and Espie did not waver from their goal.

Unfortunately when we arrived at Space Mountain, one of the most popular rides in the park, the line was very short, dashing my hopes of somehow putting off the experience a few minutes more. The line moved briskly and we quickly arrived at the boarding area. Ready or not, we were getting on the next car. In a final desperate escape attempt I asked the attendant if the ride offered a viewing area where I could virtually share in the experience while my kids rode the roller coaster. He just laughed and gently shoved me and Amelec into the front of a toboggan-like car which looked to have been designed by a deranged daredevil. Before I could get my seat belt on, my tongue was swelling and it felt as if I had a small watermelon in my mouth. It was almost impossible for me to respond when Amelec asked me "Dad, is this going to be scary?"

I did not have time to answer, as the space-age toboggan took off. What followed were a series of ups and downs, seemingly at light speed, in the dark no less. Although it was fast, the ride for me seemed to last as long as a three-day weekend. Due only to a miracle, I did not get sick. My theory is that because we were going so fast and so straight down my stomach had been compressed to the size of a thumbtack, making it impossible for any sickness whatsoever to occur. Even though I was grateful the entire contents of my most recent meal stayed inside of me, I was anxious for the ride to end. When we came to a stop and the attendant opened the door to our wicked spacecraft, I stepped on to the receiving deck, and although my head was spinning, I behaved like a man and helped my kids out of their contoured seats.

My not throwing up on Space Mountain marked the start of three days of perfect. There are not many things in life that live up to their billing, but Disneyland is one of them. From the minute we arrived to the minute we left it was like a dream. The Disneyland staff basically put on a three-day clinic on how to take care of a customer -- or in our case -- five customers. And I am proud to say that during the three days I went on most of the rides, and didn't get sick on any of them.

Most of our friends had warned us the experience would probably overwhelm our kids. Instead, the kids loved Disneyland. And so did I. We were at the park all day and most of each night. We never seemed to get tired. Maybe it is a place that turns everyone into a kid again. We went on the fast rides, the slow rides and the educational rides. We walked around for hours and held hands as we marveled at the magnificent park.

Eventually we wound up on "It's a Small World." The snail-pace boat ride, with its displays of dolls from all over the world, comes with its namesake song played in a continuous loop as you slowly drift along. It's a charming ride, although it is impossible to shake that insipid song for weeks after you disembark the ride. As I watched our kids gazing at the dolls from all over the world, it occurred to me that, in their lifetimes, the world is going to get even smaller. I wondered where Haiti fits in with our ever-globalizing society. There were no Haitian dolls on the ride, that I could see. Will Haiti ever have a place in this world, or is it forever going to be one of the world's dark corners that everyone chooses to ignore?

Later I had to beg Espie to stop singing "It's a Small World." The good news was she finally got the message, the bad news was our three days in the Magic Kingdom came to an end too soon. During the last day of our vacation we dragged our feet through the park, wishing that the day would never end. As we neared the park exit, Amelec and Espie turned to me.

"Poppa, can we go on just one more ride, please?"

"Which one?"

"SPACE MOUNTAIN!"

Figures.

We were almost out of the park, and naturally Space Mountain was on the opposite end. But if we ran and there wasn't much of a line we could probably make it work. Kathi said she would stay with Quinn. The two bigger kids and I sprinted toward Space Mountain, weaving and zigzagging our way past strollers and slow-moving pedestrians. One thing is for sure, our kids can run fast, and we made it there in rapid order. Surprisingly, I was looking forward to taking the ride with them one more time. Since I hadn't gotten nauseous the first time, I started believing I wasn't going to throw up on Space Mountain or any other ride. My mindset had changed. Believing I wasn't going to get sick meant I probably wouldn't and that really mattered to me, because I really wanted to enjoy the last roller coaster with the kids. I thought it would solidify a perfect memory of three days, not counting the annoying song from the doll ride.

As we neared the front of the line, both kids looked up at me rather sheepishly. "What's up?" I asked. We had run all of the way and we had plenty of time to enjoy the ride, I couldn't imagine what was wrong. Espie did the talking, probably because her English was a little better than Amelec's.

"Dad, would you be mad if Amelec and I went on this

ride by ourselves?"

I looked at both of them; I could tell they were nervous about asking this because they had their heads down and were rocking back and forth.

At first I was disappointed; I felt almost jilted. After all, I was their dad, and I wanted to be part of the final memory of our trip. But the more I thought about it, the more I realized how significant their request was. It wasn't that they didn't want to be with me, it was more important for them to try to fly solo. It was their way of proving they didn't need training wheels -- and how could there be a better memory than that? It was symbolic of their having gained enough confidence to go it alone as a brother and sister team. They were growing up right in front of me. It was another step in their learning to believe in themselves.

I waited with other parents at the exit of the ride. I could see them as their car raced up and down the mountain. Our kids had indeed come very far, very fast. There had been so many things to learn and understand in these first eight months. As their father, watching it all, I was proud of how they had dealt with everyday challenges. They had been extraordinarily resourceful and resilient in accepting and adapting to the new world around them. They had become American kids, and that is how they acted as they got off the ride, giggling with joy as if sharing in some grand sibling secret.

We hustled back to find Kathi and Quinn and exited the park so we could get to the airport and head home. As we left Disneyland, Amelec asked me, "Dad, is this a magic place?"

"What do you think son?"

"Yes, Dad, I think so."

"Amelec, you are right." I left it at that.

I looked back over my shoulder. Over the last eight months, I was reminded plenty of times there are a lot of magic places. Places where things happen that you thought never could, or would, happen. Magic happens when we least expect it, adding splendor to our lives. If you had asked me eight months ago if I believed in magic... well, what I can tell you is I have changed my mind about the realities of magic. What I have learned is that magic reaches beyond any of the bike rides or the roller coasters. The part that is magic is how we find ourselves in the midst of the ride.

# Chapter 17

## Two Years Later

In our home August 26th is the most important day of the year. That's the date on which we arrived in Florida, together at last as a family. We decided then to create a tradition and celebrate it every year as our "family day." It is a time to remember the distinct places we came from, and recognize the forces that aligned and brought the five of us together. It has been two years now, or 1,051,200 minutes. But it just as easily might not have happened. If certain events had been altered just slightly, even by a few minutes, we would not have become the family we are today.

It has been a remarkable journey for all of us and the transformations that have occurred in the kids, and in Kathi and me, have been nothing short of miraculous. It is amazing how fast the time has gone by. We have all changed so much. During our two-year anniversary dinner, Kathi and I reflected on the changes with Amelec and Espie. Only two years earlier we were using hand signals to communicate with them. Their English has become so advanced they were capable of engaging in a meaningful conversation and able to comprehend and appreciate the details regarding the genesis of our family. Quinn has also advanced in fast forward; he has graduated from his high chair to join us at the table as a "big boy." He even had some words to contribute to the discussion, even if only a few were understandable. But when he said the word "family" and waved his finger at all of us around the table, none of us could have said it better.

Quinn had said it, but we all felt it. Family. Over the course of the last two years we had developed a trust and a connection that felt good. But it wasn't that way in the beginning. We would all say that during our early days together, we were pretending to be a family. In reality, we were a dysfunctional group of strays that by the force of fate had somehow banded together. And when we were dysfunctional, I was at the center of the entire mess.

The early days were filled with angst. We had the paperwork and the government seals that said we were a family, so perhaps because of that we were forcing it. There were times during the first few weeks when it felt like we were in the middle of the ocean, standing on a boat that was about to capsize. But the boat slowly, day by day, righted itself. Over time, forced moments became true embraces.

The awkward anxiety of the early days finally gave way to a secure feeling we belong together. Kathi and I have taken our job as parents seriously, and once I made the decision to become a dad, I wanted to be the best dad I could be. Trying to create a constructive and positive family experience is now what Kathi and I do. The strength of the family environment is critical, for I believe kids evolve as a product of their environment. Genetics has a place in the outcome of personal development, but culture, and peers influenced by that culture, shape the mindset of every growing child. Kathi and I are intent in creating the most positive and constructive environment we can in teaching our kids solid values, life skills and character.

After two years I have learned how impressionable a young mind is. Combine the impressionable mind with the messages that are being distributed to our kids and it is frightfully easy to predict a bunch of scary outcomes. As parents, it was obvious to Kathi and I that we better go on the counterattack.

Every Monday morning I bring a "winner word" to the breakfast table. This is a word that describes the characteristics of a winner. Our children learn the word; then we use and discuss it all week long. Through the week we see how many times they can or could have put the word into action. It is a fun learning experience, and I have to say that over time our kids have become fascinated with the concept of being or becoming a winner.

We also have a list of family values we talk about on an ongoing basis. My company, just as any good company, had a mission statement describing the firm's values. As CEO I saw that the mission statement provided guiding principles my staff could refer to every day, and, most valuably, call upon during a crisis. If an organization is going to succeed, it must know what it stands for. I wanted my family to have that same benefit. So why not a family values statement? We created one for our family, and I believe discussing it, and more importantly trying to live it, have helped us become a better family

We are trying to talk to our kids now as much as we can so it becomes a habit and hopefully that habit will be an ally for us when they get older and become more exposed to the dubious values of our media-barraged society. We have good kids and it is easy to talk to them now. I do wonder how long that will last and how much of a lasting impact our efforts will ultimately have once they are inundated by the other powerful influences of friends and culture. Like all parents, all we are trying to do is construct a positive, healthy future. We know there are lots of minefields waiting for us up ahead. In the meantime we are just trying to stay prepared.

We certainly don't look like every family. We probably get different reactions than other families may get when we are out in public or enter a restaurant ... two middle aged white people with three young black kids. The beginning of our family did not happen traditionally, but the struggles we face today are no different than those facing other families. Deep down we are two parents and three kids trying to do the best we can. When I picked -- I use that term because it's the one Espie likes to use -- the kids, it was in a sense a crapshoot, as we had no idea what was at the core of their personalities. And there was a real risk they had unforeseen emotional, mental, or physical damage. This was especially true with Quinn because he was so young when I found him. The fact is

200

Kathi and I knew almost nothing about the children we brought home. But that is part of the profound paradox of adoption. Three total strangers entered our lives, dependent children who might not have made it without us, and they became family. Not friends, not acquaintances -- but family members as important to us as any blood relative. It was a miracle, really, the magic energies that brought our children to us, the family where they belong. We now feel like they have always been our kids.

We did not know if there was going to be any repercussions from their early experience with malnutrition and dehydration. Quinn was so dehydrated and so frail when I found him he was hanging onto life by a thread. Although we had no idea how these three kids were going to turn out, we just made a commitment to love them and give them the best life we could. We never assessed the situation as a risk. If it turned out that our kids came with some disabilities or some unique physical or mental challenges we were going to accept and love them for who they were, just like parents who give birth to child. I guess every parent hopes for a healthy child, but every good parent will love and support their child in any, and every condition.

Now, after two years, I can say that Amelec, Esperancia, and Quinn are very healthy and very normal. And in the same breath I can relate that they are also very unique and very exceptional.

Amelec is the jock of the family. He excels at every sport he tries. The first time he played organized soccer he made the All-Star team. At six years old he played in his first baseball game and he could switch hit from either side of the plate the entire season. He also throws any ball so well with either hand that I am sure he is ambidextrous. Socially he has come 180 degrees from that second day of school when he went limp on me in the corridor. That terrified sack of potatoes has transformed to become the alpha dog of his classmates, at least socially and athletically. He has a charm and an effervescent personality that is very appealing to everyone. He is as sweet and as caring as a kid can be.

Like all kids he has his shortcomings. While at times he is the alpha dog, at others he has the confidence of a lamb. He can be tentative, especially with some of his schoolwork when the workload is something he does not immediately understand. Sometimes his response is to shut down and quit. My sense is he will grow out of that. If I had to guess where he will be 20 years from now I would say he would be a professional athlete, but it's impossible to predict which sport -- he has performed well at all he has tried.

Twenty years from now I would guess Espie will be a scientist. Whereas Amelec has transformed 180 degrees from that moment in the corridor, Espie has transformed maybe 80 degrees from our first family dinner when she spit out Kathi's rice and beans. Espie is socially the opposite of Amelec; she is not outgoing, nor particularly gracious. She is, however, very smart and has the memory of an elephant. She is comfortable playing by herself and is curious about everything. She wants to know why things are the way they are and how things work. Simple explanations won't do -- she demands details and data. And once she knows about something she does not forget. While Amelec could be elected mayor of a town in a landslide on his personality alone, Espie walks to the beat of her own drum. I appreciate that, because I did and still do. Neither Espie nor I will win Mr. or Ms. Congeniality, but that is OK because neither of us needs to be in the center of the stage. The people who run the orphanage found Espie when she was almost two years old, skin and bones, living in a shack with dirt floors, no running water, and no electricity. When she came home with us two years ago she did not speak English. What is startling is that she now attends a private school that provides an extremely advanced curriculum and she is already recognized as one of the smartest kids in her class. Espie shows us that kids are kids, irrespective of where they are born. She reinforces the notion that if you give a kid a chance, you will find out what their potential is.

Quinn is all about potential. I have firsthand knowledge he has the strongest will of any kid on the planet. Physically he is still small, most likely due to a lack of nutrients very early on. At our last check up he was in about the 15th to 20th percentile in both height and weight for his age. While he may be small in size, his heart and will are huge, and so is his personality. Twenty years from now I would say Quinn will be a rock star, because he is extraordinarily musical and he has what is referred to in the movie business as IT, star quality charisma. It seems he was born with it. When I am with him in the supermarket people are just drawn to him. He is always singing, jabbering, dancing, or putting on a show for someone. When the car radio is tuned to rock music he plays air guitar in his car seat and sings along to all of the songs. He is not quite three, but he loves to entertain everyone.

He is still not much of a sleeper. When he wakes up in the middle of the night, he does not do what everyone else does, which is roll over and go back to sleep. He gets up, because he woke up. And once he is up, he wants company. In the dead of night, every night, maybe at two or maybe at four, the same sound echoes through our house: "Poppa!" It's as if he is serenading the household from the balcony landing area. It is his ritual, and consistent with his personality, he won't stop calling until I get up with him.

I want to be the best dad I can be. But Kathi has taken her role as a mom even more seriously. She seems to be going for the parenting All-Star team. I have never seen anyone more committed to anything as she is to being a mom. In the beginning she was exhausting herself by overdoing everything. The first few weeks our kids went to school, their afterschool snack was like a smorgasbord. Then at dinnertime she was disappointed the kids were only picking at their dinner. I had to remind her no one could possibly have an appetite for even the world's best dinner after having just stuffed themselves with the training table of snacks she had offered them.

Like the rest of us Kathi has grown and evolved. She has relaxed a little on the intensity, but she has not compromised on her promise to make a great life for these kids. She has even learned to occasionally say no, an important marker of how she has changed. She is always thinking about or doing something for the kids. Our kids are very active kids because Kathi is actively thinking up stuff for us to do.

One of Kathi's great ideas was to have us take a family

outing up to Flagstaff, where we have a cabin. Northern Arizona University is right near our little getaway house and the upcoming weekend was going to be homecoming. To celebrate, the university was having its traditional homecoming parade and a college football game featuring two undefeated teams. Having been involved in collegiate athletics I thought Kathi had a great idea for a fun and memorable time for the entire family. I made sure we bought seats outside of the student section for the game, as I know how rowdy college kids can be. But I did not think twice about the parade. After all, what could be more wholesome than sitting on the side of the street with your family watching a parade on a Saturday morning?

The homecoming parade was to start at 11 with the game to follow. We left the cabin early, as we wanted to get a good spot so the kids could see everything the parade had to offer. We had not been told the homecoming parade involved a tradition called "Sunrise services," meaning every bar along the parade route opened at six a.m. That meant partygoers would have had five hours to drink before the start of the parade. The result was NAU's version of Mardi Gras, filling the streets with an intoxicated mob by 10 a.m. It was loosely explained to me by one of the staggering participants that every one attempts to consume a week's worth of alcohol in five hours. And apparently many of them meet that goal.

So much for the wholesome family experience of watching a parade. I think we were the only five sober people in the seven square blocks of the parade route. In a pitiful coincidence that typified the scene, a very drunk young man vomited into a planter box right behind us just as the grand marshal announced, "LET THE PARADE BEGIN." Our fellow parade watchers meandered and wandered about, swearing at each other. For a few minutes a group of four or five young coeds decided to stand next to us. Their language was so vulgar and crude a sailor would have been offended. Between mentioning how cute all three of our kids were to me, they went right about shouting out their vulgarities. The crowd that lined the streets to see the parade seemed more than drunk, they seemed unstable, and my kids got a firsthand look at the ugly side of college life.

I was shocked by the behavior of the young people in the crowd, the way they dressed, how they spoke and carried themselves, and how disrespectful they were around three younger children. There was such a glaring absence of decency. None of them seemed to consider that younger kids were around.

We could not get out of there fast enough and we left the parade the minute it was over. There was one positive moment: Quinn loved a float featuring the Incredible Hulk -- he now calls the character "Green Man" and has imitated him ever since. Unfortunately the only thing that made an impact on me was the look and unbelievable behavior of the college students -- not just a few of them, but virtually all of them. I was probably as big of a knucklehead as anybody when I was in college, but sober or not; I would never have used that kind of language in front of anyone's young kids.

As we drove home to have lunch before the game, I thought to myself how college kids had changed. I had just experienced college kids today, and what I had seen was so much different than when I was in college 30 years ago. It was a herd of disrespectful slobs. It may be that it wasn't just college kids who had changed, but society that had changed. Maybe this is now who we are. I thought to myself, "Is this what we are up against? Was that a future glimpse of how our kids are going to turn out? How long will it be before they are going to pierce their nose to jam a ring through it? When will they want their first tattoo? And, even worse, will a day come when they lose respect for those around them? Will a day come when they lose respect for themselves?"

While the parade was a drunken festival for the students, it was a sobering experience for me. It reminded me that it will be less than a dozen years before Amelec and Espie are off to college. Quinn won't be far behind. Could our kids turn out different than the college kids I saw today? Would they, or could they become leaders and abstain from being the followers who get swept up in the dangerous current of mainstream culture? And what will pop culture be like 15 years from now? Our innocent and little kids won't be little or innocent for long. It is just a matter of time before they will find their place in this world, in one form or another.

I thought about the desperate life that was behind them, in that broken country we had delivered them from. I started to think about and compare that to all of the complex choices that will soon be in front of them in this country. I had to wonder whether our kids just witnessed an environment worse than the one they had come from. By the time we had arrived back home, I had moved up in the parenting club, because I had begun to worry about the future.

We finished lunch and headed back to NAU to watch the game. Based on the experience in the morning I braced myself for the worst. I almost decided to cancel and just take the kids down to the park. We had made one smart move -- we had bought good seats and when we got there we were surrounded by adults who were interested in watching the game. They also appeared to have skipped the traditional sunrise services. Just before the game started, three college students worked their way across the aisle and sat down in seats right in front of us. Uh oh, I thought. Here we go again.

But during the first quarter we ended up getting acquainted with them: Two guys and a girl, the polar opposite of what I had seen just hours before. They weren't drunk or obnoxious; in fact, I would describe them as classy. I asked them why they were sitting over here and not in the student section, and they said they preferred these seats -- season tickets belonging to their parents -- because over here they could watch the game. They were polite and very gracious as they interacted with our kids. We learned that one of them was studying to become a teacher because he loved kids and he thought he could make a difference in the world by becoming a teacher. He said he also felt there were not many people in his generation who were interested in becoming teachers.

It was a great football game, and our kids enjoyed watching the cheerleaders and the pageantry and even the game itself. And during the game we had made three new friends. The three students gracefully rearranged some of my earlier thinking. This was the other side of the coin, one I am thrilled our kids got to see. The home team lost the game, but the afternoon was a win for me. That morning I had witnessed a scene lacking in common decency, but in the afternoon I had experienced an abundance of decency in the three college students who sat in front of us. They gave me some hope.

That night after I put the kids to bed I sat on the deck at our cabin and watched the moon come up. The events of the day and the contrasting examples of young adults I had experienced had given me plenty to think about. I stared into the sky and asked; what is the destiny of Amelec, Espie and Quinn? How much do I help shape their destiny as their dad? Or is their destiny already predetermined, and I can only patiently watch as the winds of the change blow by? Was it destiny that brought us together in the first place, or was it just random luck? Or did I want all of this to happen, and need all of this to happen, so I made it happen?

These last two years have produced a very unexpected journey, and a dramatic transformation in the five of us. If you had told me, even just a few short years ago, one night I would be sitting on this deck thinking about the future of three young kids -- my three young kids -- I would have said you were crazy. Einstein said there are two ways to live your life. One is as though nothing is a miracle. The other is as though everything is a miracle. I couldn't count all the chances or choices that have brought me to this point and have formed what has become my destiny. I also couldn't tell you that some of this wasn't a miracle.

So as I sat on that deck and thought about the future of our kids I had plenty of reasons to be optimistic, and I had plenty of reasons to worry. None of us can predict or control our destiny. Things happen and sometimes we find the strength to deal with them. So as the night got longer and the moon drifted higher in the sky, I realized it was foolhardy to spend time worrying about how or why any of this happened. I took a deep breath and stared off into the expanding night accepting that the unexpected does happen. And I am glad it did.

# Epilogue
## Hey, What About Me?

More than two decades have passed since the Friday afternoon when I had the vasectomy. At the time, it was an easy decision. As I walked out of the doctor's office, not knowing what laid ahead for me, I believed I had gained at least one certainty -- I was not going to become a dad.

Now that I am a dad, I am learning to understand many of the things that come with the role. I also understand how flawed my thinking was 20 years ago. I had said no to something before I understood what I was saying no to. Now it is easy to look back and realize how close I came to cheating myself out of one of the most wondrous experiences a man can have. I don't know if I was destined to become a dad or if I simply got lucky. In either case I arrived at parenthood by a linked chain of circumstances some would call fate. I showed up late to the parenting party, and came in through the back door.

It is easy for me to describe the sum of my experience as a dad. Eighty percent of the time I find parenting to be a joyous and enriching experience and in the process I have discovered a heartbeat inside of me that I did not know existed. And, the other 20 percent of the time ... I want to slit my wrists. The experience, while mostly positive, has not been easy.

Over the last two years many people have commented that Kathi and I have done a noble and decent thing by adopting Espie, Amelec and Quinn. It is true we probably saved their lives, and it is undeniable we have dramatically improved their lives. They now have choices, options, possibilities and a future. They would have had none of those things if they had stayed in Haiti, assuming they even survived. So, we intervened in three lives and profoundly changed them, although we don't look at our experience of parenting in those terms.

But if there is a prime beneficiary in all of this, it's me. I am the one who got a second chance, a chance to comprehend the love a man can only experience as a father. Until I became a dad I did not fully understand what love was. Years ago when I was lying in that doctor's office I did not realize what I was willing to walk away from. Now I know. Now I realize I was given a chance to learn about love the hard way.

And I did not know I had it in me.

I will tell you that I would not trade being a dad to Amelec, Espie and Quinn for anything in this world.

That doesn't mean I sometimes don't think about my old life, especially on the difficult days when one of our kids is driving me crazy. But my old life is just that. In my old life I swore I would never reside in the kind of neighborhood where we now live: Unlike the estate-like street where Kathi and I used to live, it's classic family suburbia, complete with parks on the street corners and jungle gyms in the yards. Instead of Bentleys and Ferraris, tricycles crowd these streets. Moving here was the final goodbye to the old life. The quality of my life is no longer defined by extravagant houses or cars or any of the other meaningless stuff. The quality of my life is now defined by Amelec, Espie, and Quinn, and being a parent to them with Kathi. In my old life, one of my halfhearted goals was to become a scratch golfer, which, for the record, I never achieved. Now my goal is to become a scratch dad. And there is nothing halfhearted in that pursuit.

After two years of parenthood, I can't say I am a better man for the experience. The only person qualified to say something like that about me is Kathi. I can say that being a dad has changed me. When our kids first came home, I spent more moments than I am proud of worried and stressed out that the kids were going to break one of our antiques or pieces of art as they ran around the house. Now I only worry they'll break one of their bones. Our house is no longer filled up with antiques and showpieces; instead it is filled with the upbeat energy and laughter of three great kids. It has been transformed from a house to a home. And I, too, have been transformed. My ego has shrunk and my sense of humanity has grown. We gave the kids their new life, and, in return, they gave us ours.

When Kathi and I began our adoption process, although I could have qualified as the least likely guy on the planet to adopt three kids, we went ahead and did it anyway. It has been demanding and challenging, much more difficult than I had imagined. It has also been the best experience of my life. And if I can pull it off -- even really enjoy it -- anyone can.

I only wish this story of hope might inspire you to consider the possibilities of becoming an adoptive parent. Kids are kids, whether they are from Helena or Haiti. All kids, irrespective of the circumstance they were born into, need a hand to hold on to, someone to love them and help them find their way. There are too many kids in this world who are alone. Today, millions of orphaned or abandoned kids need someone to give them a loving home.

I would like to hang around longer and tell you more, but I have to run. Amelec has a soccer game this morning and Espie has a dance recital early this afternoon. I will be at both events cheering them on with Quinn by my side. In my new life, there is nothing I would rather be doing.

# Photographs

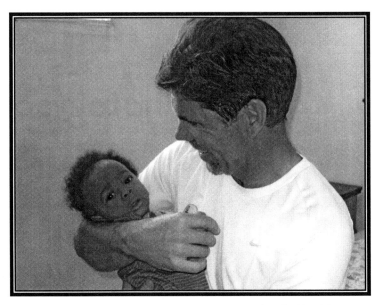

Quinn and me at the orphanage 2 months after finding him.
April 2006

Kathi, Amelec and Espie in Haiti before the adoptions were
finalized. April 2006

An early family photo about two months after bringing the kids
home. October 2006

Quinn celebrating our first anniversary of family day.
August 2007

Espie (age 6) and me
November 2007

Amelec turns 8 years old.
January 2009

Quinn loves music (age 2.5).
August 2008

Halloween.
October 2008

My 54<sup>th</sup> Birthday Celebration.
December 2008

Juntunen family,
December 2009

# Acknowledgements

Writing this book has been a labor of love; years from now our three kids will have something that memorializes how we became a family. I have to thank two people for making this book a reality. The first is Brian Curtis, who gave me the shove, inspiring me to start writing. Without his encouragement this book never would have happened. The second person I want to thank is the executive editor of the book, Tripp Baltz. Few readers ever see the before and after version of a book, and since in this case that is true, you will have to trust me on this. Tripp's many contributions made this book better. A lot better! I am very grateful for his intelligent rearranging of some very awkward sentences. More importantly I am appreciative for his passionate commitment to the cause that fueled this project. By the way Tripp and his wife, Kris are also adoptive parents. A few years ago I started out with an idea to write a book, and along the way made at least two new friends. The way I see things there is no better byproduct of any activity than friendship. May this book produce new friends and acquaintances for many people as time goes on.

# References

*Chapter 2:*
Sigmund Freud quote from "Brainy Quote,"
http://www.brainyquote.com/quotes/quotes/s/sigmun
dfre165464.html

*Chapter 3:*
Lyrics from the Pink Floyd song "Breathe," *Dark Side of the Moon*, 1973. Found at Pink Floyd Lyrics,
http://www.pink-floyd-lyrics.com/html/breathe-dark-lyrics.html

*Chapter 7:*
U.S. State Department statistics on international adoptions found at "Total Adoptions to the U.S.,"
http://adoption.state.gov/news/total_chart.html.

*Chapter 16:*
"The Happiest Place on Earth," from the Disneyland Resort web site,
http://disneyland.disney.go.com/disneyland/en_US/pa
rks/overview?name=DisneylandResortParksOverviewPa
ge&bhcp=1

*Chapter 17:*
Albert Einstein quote from "Brainy Quote,"
http://www.brainyquote.com/quotes/authors/a/albert
_einstein.html

# About the Author

Craig Juntunen's life experience can be broken into three distinct eras ...

In his early life he was involved heavily in athletics, playing quarterback for a total of 14 seasons. He finished his athletic career as a quarterback in the Canadian Football League. He was elected into the State of Idaho Athletic Hall of Fame and the University of Idaho Hall of Fame.

His experience as a leader on the football field led to his developing into an entrepreneur. He successfully built and sold a company with a very successful track record and temporarily retired.

His experience as a quarterback and as an entrepreneur blended together to form philanthropic passions. He has been involved in many charitable giving efforts, and until recently his most notable achievement was launching the Chances for Children foundation.

In May 2010 he started the Both Ends Burning Campaign, a project to change the landscape of international adoption. He and his wife Kathi live in Scottsdale, Arizona with their three children, Amelec, Espie and Quinn. Craig is a recognized expert on international adoption and a frequently sought out public speaker. Please visit www.bothendsburning.org to learn more about the campaign or to set up a speaking engagement with Craig.

CPSIA information can be obtained at www.ICGtesting.com
Printed in the USA
BVOW03s1203271013

334695BV00003B/16/P

9 781432 734862